UNLOCATING

*How Undoing Everything You Think
Will Bring True Freedom*

By Margie Lundy

ISBN: 9781097971633
Cover design by Cassie Ward, www.cassiecollective.com.
Photograph by Margie Lundy, somewhere in Wyoming, 2010.
Margie Lundy, PO Box 732, Tavares, FL 32778

For a **free** guide, "Where to Start on the Road to Freedom", visit www.unlocating.com.

CONTENTS

INTRODUCTION

Sometimes the American dream is not so dreamy. Do you ever feel stuck, tired, or bored with your life? Do you long for freedom, without running away? Or do you long to run away? Have you looked at everything you thought would bring you freedom and wondered if everything you thought was wrong?

You will find true freedom by undoing everything you think. This book is for anyone who wonders if there is another way. It will help you rethink some key areas and show you that another way isn't only possible, but it's possible for you. You will realize if the Lundys can do this, anyone can!

As a family of nomads, we've explored the country for the past nine years with our rolling home. We've schooled from home for the past eleven. We've worked from home for the past fifteen. So we've found a lot of freedom, no matter where our home was. And we've undone a lot of our thinking in order to find it. We've been blessed to help many rethink location, education, business, health and more. In this book, you will learn how to undo your thinking, look at life differently, and know there is help along the way.

You don't have to hit the road and change your entire life to find freedom either. You can read this book and start rethinking some of these areas today. You can implement changes tomorrow or over the next few years. Our family has complete freedom now and rethinking everything is how we started. I promise if you undo everything you think, you will find true freedom in every area of your life. Even if you undo just a few of the things you think, you will find freedom in those areas. And I guarantee the smallest taste of freedom will leave you wanting more. It's out there and it's worth simply undoing what you think.

Don't miss out on the freedom you desire, wishing you had

the same opportunities as others. Be the person who rethinks and reconsiders everything. Then inspire people to go after their dreams, because you went after yours. Start today. The lessons in this book will show you how to begin. The stories will show you why it's worth it. Each chapter will give you another area to re-consider. If you are ready to pursue true freedom, all you have to do is keep reading. Take control of your life and make it the life of your dreams.

CHAPTER 1: UNKNOWN

Believe it or not, unlocating probably isn't the craziest thing we've done. My husband, Allen, and I have always craved the freedom to step out into the unknown. We moved away for work, while others stayed close to family and friends. We adopted all three of our children, while our friends were having babies. We helped plant a new church, while others attended long-established ones. We slowed our life down, while others were speeding up. We built a new business, while that industry didn't exist yet. We homeschooled our kids, while there was a great school just down the road. So when I proposed the idea of full-time RVing, Allen wasn't surprised and quickly agreed. We both got excited, and though we had no idea how to make it happen, it would simply be our next adventure of seeking freedom in the unknown.

We've seen so much as we've traveled the last nine years together. Our cast of characters includes my husband Allen, our daughter Lizzy, our sons Josh and Matt, and our dog Jack. Allen craves adventure and has led our family into countless, sometimes questionable exploits, that mostly turned out great. Josh, nineteen, is a US Marine, currently stationed in Hawaii, who we are extremely proud of and miss greatly. Lizzy, nineteen, is currently working and getting ready to strike out on her own in Nevada. Matt, seventeen, is weighing his future options and enjoying his last year of rock climbing across the country. Jack is a dog. He takes naps. And I'm Margie. I hold all of this together and make the things happen. Hi, it's nice to meet you. We'd love to join you around a campfire one day.

Many of these adventures into the unknown we started alone, but we always found help. Slowly, but surely, others interested in the same ideas would start appearing. This happened everywhere, every time, with every location, industry, theme, or topic. We noticed that in every new thing we experienced, a group of helpers would begin to gather around us. I think they're best described as a tribe, which Merriam-Webster defines as "a group of persons having a common character, occupation, or interest."[1] Sometimes this tribe had the answers, but not always. Sometimes they were searching for them too. Sometimes, like us, they didn't even know what questions to ask. But they were seeking freedom in the unknown too. They were the trailblazers.

This tribe very often had not even formed yet. Back then, there wasn't a support group for adoption, church planting, or RVing with kids, where we could simply sign up for a newsletter. Many were out blazing their own trails, just like we were, until we eventually found our way together. We first noticed this with fellow adoptive parents, also looking for answers to challenges that traditional families didn't face. That tribe helped us navigate unmapped territory and supported us in radical ways. This community wasn't necessarily our neighbors, though sometimes our neighbors were part of it. It wasn't just our nomadic friends, our fellow entrepreneurs, or other unschooling families. It was a group that formed specifically for this purpose and for this point in time, to help each other in this unknown adventure.

Today, many of these tribes do continue to exist as support groups, ready and waiting for you to sign up for their newsletters! If you're looking for one, I'll be glad to introduce you. If your new adventure already has a supportive tribe, you are very fortunate to have such a valuable resource as you get started. But rest assured, if you step out into a completely new unknown tomorrow, you won't be alone for long. Your tribe of trailblazers will come.

When looking for answers, most things can (and should!) be googled first. Although some people like to ask, it's very easy to search for the answers. Open google.com, type a phrase, and click enter. Or just ask Siri. But very often, when someone posts online that they bought a widget, immediately you see, "What is a widget?" Google it. "Where can I get a widget?" Google it. "How much is a widget?" Please, google it. That's obviously a pet peeve of mine. Then, there are the people who join a group about a specific subject, and post, "Hi, I'm new. Tell me everything you know about this subject." You know who you are, and I love you, but maybe you could reconsider that. The entire group exists because that subject is too big to explain in one comment. Blogs are created about that subject. Books are written to cover it. The answers are already there, just waiting for you. Pull up your chair, get comfortable, and read a little before asking your (now more informed) question. I'll admit, I'm easily annoyed. :)

Sometimes, though, there are questions that just don't seem to have answers. Even worse, there are times when it's hard to figure out what question to ask. How do you correctly word, "Is it okay if we sell our house and live in an RV, traveling the country with our children or is that going to ruin their lives and land us in jail?" I googled that exact phrase out of curiosity and the results were irrelevant, strange, or a little scary. When we first started thinking about nomadic life, we began searching. But as we had not heard the phrase "nomadic life" yet, it wasn't an easy process. Fortunately, we started finding the trailblazers.

People everywhere are waiting to help, if you only pay attention. I demonstrated this to our daughter Lizzy once in a hardware store. We were out shopping and Allen called to see if we could buy a coupling while we were out. I didn't know what a coupling was, but he said they were at Home Depot in the plumbing section. Because I'm an intelligent, strong woman, I knew I could walk into that store, check all the aisle signs to find the correct one, and scan all the items down each row until we found something that said coupling. Because I was exhausted from shopping all day with Lizzy, who is an Olympic-level marathon-shopper, I just didn't want to. I could have googled it too, but instead I decided it was time for her to learn more about our power as women. I'm sorry if you're a feminist. Maybe skip to the next paragraph. As we walked into the store, I said "Just follow my lead and act confused." Since she had no idea what I was doing, she didn't have to act. I stopped in the middle front, looking helplessly between the piece of paper I held that said coupling and a random aisle sign. About thirty seconds later, an employee in an orange apron rushed over to see if he could help us. About sixty seconds later, I had a coupling in my hand. Maybe that doesn't sound like a great power to you, but ninety seconds in a store with Lizzy is pretty much superhuman.

This doesn't just happen for women, though. I've spent a lot of time, mostly bored, in hardware stores across the country waiting on Allen. So many times an employee, or often just a friendly customer, will sidle up and say, "So, you working on some plumbing?" Then they will compare parts, share experiences, and swap what I'm sure are very fascinating stories about plumbing. I usually wander off. One time, I left him in the fishing section for an hour and shopped for groceries. When I came back, he was excited about all the inside information he had received about the local fishing, including where to go and what bait worked best. I said, "So the employees here know their stuff?" He said, "Oh no, it was just some guy wearing camo." People love to help.

Why this help always comes or how it works is beyond me. Is it simply the Law of Attraction? Or more likely the Law of Vibration? According to Bob Proctor, "The vibration you're in is going to dictate what you attract into your life."[2] In other words, you're operating on a certain frequency, so the tribe that is pulled to you is on the same frequency. However it works, I just know it does. Maybe one day people will quote Margie Lundy saying, "Your tribe of trailblazers will come." It will probably be something really lame instead. Hopefully I will attract a tribe of authors who are thriving despite having only lame sayings quoted from their books.

We've learned so many things on and off the road and we love sharing them. Even though we are homeschooling our kids, I'm certain that Allen and I have learned even more. We've found so much freedom, in so many different areas, that we are passionate about helping others find it too. We've blazed many trails ourselves, but more importantly, we have been blessed by the help and support of other trailblazers.

Two things have helped us actually enjoy the unknown. You don't have to do it perfectly. And you don't have to know everything before you begin. Perfectionism leads to anxiety and that desire for all the knowledge leads to overwhelm. First, we don't want either of those outcomes. Secondly, we realize both are impossible to attain anyway. We just act and never worry about perfection, which is probably why we never worry. Do bad things happen? Certainly! But since we assume things will not go perfectly, those bad things are expected. And you simply can't know everything in the beginning. You can research for days or years, but you will always have more to learn along the way. Things will change, as will you. Sometimes you just have to step out into the unknown. Don't wait for the perfect time. We hear this so often from the retirees in our campgrounds. They wish they had started traveling years ago, when they were younger and more able to enjoy it. Don't put if off until *someday* when you are completely ready. You might just *someday* yourself out of a life.

I've wanted to write this book for years. When I finally started, though, I didn't take my own advice. I wanted to know all the details first, such as publishing, marketing, advertising, designing, etc. I was procrastinating the book until I had the rest all figured out. I finally realized I just needed to write. I needed to take the step of finishing the book. Then I would learn the rest later. If I never wrote the book, the rest wouldn't matter anyway. That is how most of our life has gone. We had to take the steps and learn the rest later. That's helped us step into the unknown to find true freedom.

I wrote this book about the freedom we've found and the lessons we've learned, in hopes of sharing the freedom, while sparing you the lessons. The stories are all true, though I may have omitted a few details to avoid prosecution or humiliation, and they're included so you can laugh at us and along with us. It's totally fine, because we get a kick out of that too!

This is not a how-to book, but more of a why-to. Though there are many resources included, each chapter's how-to would require an entire book. Maybe that endeavor is in our future, if there's a need for it. Who knows? For now, that is just another unknown.

Here are a few things to keep in mind as you read:

·I don't think I am an expert in any of these areas, though I can point you to some.

·I don't think our way is the best way. It's just the best way for our family at this time.

·I don't think you need to do everything we do. Do what's best for your family at this time. You do you.

·I don't think you'll like everything I say. But if you like everything you read in every book you read, you're reading the wrong books.

·I do think you'll be surprised with how much freedom unthinking these things can bring.

·I do think you'll be inspired to dream a little bigger. If the Lundys can, truly anyone can.

·I do think you'll be impressed we're all still alive, intact, and mostly well-adjusted members of society.

·I do think you'll wonder if it's fair for one family to have so much fun. It certainly is, and you can too!

CHAPTER 2: UNLOCATING

For the past nine years, our family has lived on the road, exploring the country as full-time RVers. We are so grateful for our nomadic life and the freedom we've found. We've traveled through forty-nine states (so far), visited over seventy national parks and monuments, seen countless other amazing places, and met thousands of inspiring people. We do whatever we want, wherever we want, whenever we want, which is indeed as cool as it sounds. We might choose between climbing in the northwest or hiking in the southwest. Or the choice might be visiting family in the northeast or the southeast. No matter what we choose, we can't lose. Our life is a series of choices between two awesome things.

What? Why? How? You probably have a lot of questions, as did all of our family and friends as we shared our crazy plan to hit the road. In January of 2010, we considered relocating for many reasons. We already worked from home and homeschooled our kids. As many Ohioans do, my parents retired and moved to Florida. And like the retirees, we were really tired of Ohio winters. It is no coincidence this decision happened in January. The problem was we couldn't decide where to move to. During long drives, we used to love playing the game "If we could move anywhere, where would we go?" Once that became a reality and we actually could move anywhere, it wasn't as fun, because we simply didn't know. There were so many good options, but how would we choose just one?

On a whim, I mentioned we loved camping, so we could just live in our camper until we could decide. Immediately the wheels began spinning, figuratively in the beginning, and we realized we really could. As long as we had an internet signal, we could be anywhere and still work. We started asking each other if we were allowed to do that. Then we asked why on earth we would need permission. Then we started dreaming of all the places we could go and it was decided, pretty much that same day.

We took a few weeks to research and plan, before we announced our idea. We took a few more weeks to find a great truck. Yes, it was painful to trade a new truck and a new van straight up for an old truck! We took a few more weeks to find the perfect RV. No, it wasn't painful to trade in our little travel trailer for a giant fifth wheel. Then we took a few months to prepare, purge, organize, pack, and sell. We moved into the RV, right in the driveway. Yes, it was a little painful to watch all of our possessions sold in an estate sale. But at least it only lasted a few hours, we were no longer attached to our stuff, and we were thousands of dollars richer.

Here are some answers to your probable questions, and many questions we received as we launched.

•No, we were not desperate. We were living the "American dream" and found it a little boring.

•No, we were not rich. We worked online with internet, phones, computers, printers, and a home office.

•No, we were not poor. We had great jobs and a great house, but also a great dream to travel.

•No, we didn't yank the kids out of school. Well, we did years ago, because we already homeschooled.

•No, we didn't need all that stuff. We love the saying, the more stuff you own, the more stuff owns you. We don't miss any of it.

•No, we were not crazy. Okay, maybe we were. But we still are, and it works for us!

We knew it was the opportunity of a lifetime and we were grateful to be able to do it. Instead of just teaching the kids about this country, they would get to see it. They would also get to visit family from Florida to Alaska.

We would give up a house, but gain an ever-changing backyard. We would miss our family, friends, neighbors, and church family, but we could go make memories while still keeping in touch.

At first, we were a little sad to leave our house in Troy, Ohio, because we thought we had finally found our last home. It was the perfect little farmhouse, with a giant yard, a big garage, a fun tree house, and acres of cornfields on every side. It was out in the country, but close to town. Allen had just finished his workshop and his man cave. The kids had a secret playroom in the attic. We had remodeled, redecorated, and finally just bought the huge, leather, sectional couch we'd wanted for ten years. But once the dream of travel began to grow, we quickly let go of the dream house.

As we got closer to our launch date, I was still madly researching, trying to find all the obscure details that are readily available today. Mail, school, insurance, healthcare, pets, WiFi, and campgrounds were all unknowns. I found a few inspiring families who were on the road and had blogs. It was fun to read about their adventures and know we wouldn't be completely alone. But we were still mostly alone in figuring out the next steps. We worked through it though, and slowly but surely, those trailblazers came along.

We launched on May 5, 2010 and drove through our beautiful town of Troy one last time before heading east. I may have cried. But ask my kids, I always cry. I was just grateful for the time and friends we had there, and excited about our new adventure. Before we left, we stopped at Walmart for a few more supplies. We figured we might as well get used to it, since Walmart stores are a popular overnight stop for RVers. (That has certainly proven true over the years!) On the way out of the parking lot, our back jack managed to snag a bag of salt, which we discovered a mile down the road. So we left a mark on the town and learned our first of many lessons.

We went to Pennsylvania and then West Virginia for some kayaking, which is what we would have done anyway. We usually camped on the weekends with our Ohio whitewater club, but we no longer had to go home for the weekdays. It was really fun adventuring as a family all week and then seeing our friends again on the weekends. After a month, we decided to head west for parts unknown. We explored Indiana, Michigan, Wisconsin, west to Oregon, north to Washington, and south to California. Then we headed back east, all the way to Ohio, and south to Florida for the winter. You can read about every adventure along the way on our website at www.unlocating.com.

So yes, we hit twenty-five states in those first eight months and yes, that was way too much and way too fast, in case you were wondering. That was another lesson we learned. Slow down. We hit a wall and stopped appreciating all the awesome places. We were exhausted, unimpressed, and quite grouchy with each other. If you plan to hit the road for just a year-long road trip, you might prefer to squeeze more in. But if you plan to travel indefinitely, like us, slow down so you have time to soak it all in. Get out of vacation mode as soon as you can. Cook your normal meals instead of convenient, travel food. Schedule work days and downtime, because it's hard to fit those in when you're constantly surrounded by enticing sights. We began to stay for a week or two in the middle of nowhere, purposefully away from anything tempting. We needed time to work, plan, catch up, organize, clean, and rest. The kids needed time to just be kids, read, climb trees, play, fight, get bored, and all the normal things they did when we were not exploring fascinating places. Once our pace slowed down, we started appreciating everything more. We also started appreciating each other more!

We're now known as nomads, digital nomads, full-time RVers, full-time families, location-independent entrepreneurs, xscapers, working-age RVers, and more. But when we first hit the road, we weren't known at all. People were familiar with retired full-time RVers and families vacationing in RVs, but there were few families like us. There were some clubs for retirees, and campground events on the weekends for families, but very little for us. We found the trailblazers, though. We would meet a family occasionally and trade helpful advice, share a meal, or enjoy stories around a campfire. As we traveled, posting our experiences online, more of the tribe slowly came together.

In January of 2011, we attended our first rally with other full-time families. There were fifteen families, and that was the extent of the traveling families we knew. We all parked in a circle and the kids ran wild in the center, having the times of their lives. The girls traveled in a giant pack, giggling and squealing all day. The boys looked a little like Lord of the Flies. But it was beautiful seeing so many kids enjoying their freedom together. The adults shared meals, campfires, and conversations, having the times of our lives as well. We weren't quite as feral as the children, but it was certainly refreshing spending so much time with like-minded travelers. We had a science day, movie night, business expo, RV prizes, singing with guitars and percussion, and so much more. It was wonderful being surrounded by our tribe, though it was small. Recently, we enjoyed another rally, this time with over EIGHTY families. And those were just the families who signed up in the first few days, because there were limited spots available! Over the past nine years, we've met hundreds of RVing families in person, and we know of thousands more online. So the scene is definitely changing as mobile jobs are increasing. There is so much help available today. The tribe of full-time families is definitely established and ready to assist you, complete with newsletters.

RV life tends to confuse some people, so let me clear up a few things. We have a very small home, but we don't go without. We go with everything! And we take it wherever we want. Imagine taking a vacation and not having to pack, because you bring your home with you. That is pretty much our life in a nutshell, except the vacation never ends. Also, it's not a vacation, because we bring our daily life with us.

For those interested in specific details, we live in a four hundred square foot fifth wheel RV with three bedrooms and two bathrooms. While we also have two offices, those share space with a bedroom and a kitchen/living room. We have all the typical conveniences of a house, including power, water, sewer, refrigerator, stove, oven, microwave, sinks, shower, hot water heater, air conditioner, furnace, ceiling fan, fireplace, satellite, and three televisions. While you might not have needed that list, we still meet people who wonder if we have heat, how we cook, or where we shower. We get offers of hot meals, which I cook every day, though we never turn down free food. And we've had many invitations to stay with friends, too, but we prefer our comfy, king-size bed in our own bedroom. We always appreciate the sentiment; we just love our tiny home.

When we launched, we quickly learned that people have some interesting misconceptions about RV life. It's getting better these days, with mobile jobs becoming more prevalent. But back in 2010, when it wasn't as common, we were amazed at the responses we received. When people heard we lived in an RV, they usually assumed one of two things: we were independently wealthy or we were basically destitute. There was no middle ground, which is where we actually fell of course.

At our very first national park, our children, who were ten, ten, and seven at the time, were very excited about our new life. When a ranger asked them where they were from, they gladly shared they lived in an RV. The compassionate ranger did the pity head tilt and said "Oh, you poor things." Our kids had no idea why she was sad. Of course I understood, so I stepped in and explained how we travel the country full time. The now-snooty ranger actually did the nose in the air move and said "It must be nice having that kind of money." Our kids again were confused by her tone. Of course I understood this as well. As sarcasm is my love language (which you'll hopefully learn in this book), I adopted the same snooty attitude and said, "Yes, it is." Our kids had no idea what happened to either of us and just wanted their Junior Ranger badges.

Back at home, in the comfy RV we all love, we explained how the ranger assumed one thing and then another. We talked about how to best answer the very common questions of where they were from and where they live. We shared how many people wouldn't understand life on the road, but we could graciously help them see how awesome it was. So at the next national park, when a ranger asked where they were from, all three kids at once launched into our life story of RVing, traveling, how amazing it was, what we've seen, what we've done, how we still have jobs, and how we're not poor, but we're not rich. It was a very entertaining, very long conversation with that unfortunate ranger. At home again, and over the next few weeks, we discussed and honed those answers. The rangers and others were usually interested and impressed, which led to great conversations, instead of pity and judgment.

As an aside, this answer did get a little more difficult for Josh when he joined the Marines. During boot camp, a drill instructor asked where he was from and Josh hesitated. As you would expect, his drill instructor gave him a hard time about not knowing this basic information. Josh, in his overly-talkative kind of way, yelled "Drill Instructor, I was born in Ukraine, lived in Ohio, am a Florida resident, with land in Arkansas, but we travel full time in an RV, so I'm not sure how to answer, Drill Instructor!" Josh said his DI just turned around and walked away. Maybe he was just processing all of those details, but I have a feeling he was hiding a smile.

As we settled into a normal life of traveling, some themes naturally developed for each year on the road. For the first year, we concentrated on national parks and monuments. We loved the Junior Ranger program, which taught us all about the park, area, and features. The kids have over seventy badges and patches all over their green Junior Ranger vests, which was really fun as we entered new parks. The kids would strut around, while the rangers praised their efforts and tourists took their pictures. They're less excited to see any parks these days, but as teens, they don't get excited about much. But we especially enjoyed the Badlands, Yellowstone, Grand Tetons, Crater Lake, Mt. Rainier, Yosemite, Death Valley, Zion, and the Everglades.

The next year we focused on amusement, specifically amusement parks. We bought Cedar Fair season passes, which included Kings Island in Ohio, Carowinds in North and South Carolina, Kings Dominion in Virginia, Worlds of Fun in Missouri, and Knott's Berry Farm in California. It was so convenient to have our home in the parking lot. It was fun to stay until closing time, park at a nearby store to sleep, and then come right back in the morning. We still hit a few national parks on our route, because they were too good to miss. We've sprinkled those in every year, no matter the theme. That second year we explored Williamsburg, Kitty Hawk, Washington D.C., Gateway Arch, Petrified Forest, Grand Canyon, and White Sands. Each year we also attended rallies and met with other traveling families, because we love our nomadic community. That summer, we were headed to Maine, but took a detour to Joplin, Missouri, which I'll share more about in the unscheduling chapter.

Also during this second year, Allen reached his goal of watching a game at every Major League Baseball stadium! It started in Cincinnati and took him sixteen years, but he finished in San Diego in September of 2011. We even hit two games in Canada on our honeymoon! Yes, I am that awesome. We'd gone on road trips together and he'd taken many trips with his buddies, but our mobile life made it a little easier to finish the list. The whole family hit Arizona in August for the next to last stadium. In case you're wondering, his favorite was Wrigley Field. He likes the nostalgia of the old ballparks and also loved Fenway Park and Tiger Stadium.

Year three we called "When in Rome" and we sought out the local favorites. We discovered Cheerwine in North Carolina, which is similar to cherry Coke. We also found a filming location from The Hunger Games movie at Triple Falls. In Lancaster County, Pennsylvania, we looked beyond the touristy Amish shops in town and found great roadside stands. We spent a lot of time at Hershey's Chocolate World in Pennsylvania. I would feel guilty, but "When in Rome!" Fresh lobster in Maine was awesome, as was Acadia National Park. In New York City, we saw as many sights as we could possibly squeeze in. The kids liked seeing places they'd seen on TV, and they loved the pizza, bagels, and pretzels. We spent a lot of time kayaking, rafting, and shredding in West Virginia and Pennsylvania. In Georgia, we toured the Chick-fil-A corporate headquarters, which was both fascinating and yummy. In Louisiana, we visited Duck Commander of Duck Dynasty fame. Our route also took us to Gettysburg, Plymouth Rock, Niagara Falls, and the Flight 93 Memorial.

Our fourth was a year of hunting. We were on a mission to hit our last contiguous state and to find some land. We didn't want to settle down. We just wanted a campground away from the campgrounds, so Allen and the boys could hunt, the kids and dog could run, and we could all just relax away from everything. We finally hit state number forty-eight, North Dakota. We went simply to put the sticker on our map, but we loved Theodore Roosevelt National Park. It was like the Badlands, but with greenery. In Montana, we got to hang out with the Budweiser Clydesdales. And we finally went to Glacier National Park, a place we'd missed because it was so far out of the way. We continued west to Idaho searching for land, but then changed directions and headed to Arkansas. There we found Lundy Mountain in the Ozarks. You'll learn more about that in the chapter about homesteading, or unhomesteading, since it was anything but typical.

Most of our fifth year was spent in Arkansas on the homestead, unhomesteading. We learned so much there, raising, growing, and hunting our own food. While we planned to brave a winter there, after the first snow we decided to head south to Florida. The snow was pretty, and fun for a day, but we just don't do cold anymore. Southern winters have spoiled us. We spent much of that magical winter at the Wizarding World of Harry Potter at Universal Studios and Islands of Adventure. Wintering in Florida has some great perks!

We spent the majority of year six on the homestead again, but instead of being fun, it started becoming work. Plus, the hitch itch started hitting us. It's a real struggle for nomads. The first year was new and exciting. We had so much to learn and build. The animals were cute and cuddly. The second year was good, but tiring. We knew what to do and were just completing chores. The animals were still cute, but they required a lot of care. So we headed to Texas for the winter and found renters who would enjoy Lundy Mountain more.

During year seven, it was all about adventure. We were ready for the freedom of the open road. We were also getting healthy again, and realized these two things were directly related. I'll explain that in the chapter about undieting. We explored Texas and New Mexico, including Padre Island, Big Bend, and Carlsbad Caverns, three places we'd skipped because they were out of the way. Then we had a blast in Arizona and Utah, with our friends and fellow nomads, Hyrum and Tiana Johnson and their family. We hiked in many parks, Grand Canyon North, Zion, Arches, Bryce Canyon, Canyonlands, Cedar Breaks, and Grand Staircase-Escalante. While the Johnsons headed north, we headed east to Colorado. We explored quaint mountain towns, drove to the top of Mount Evans and Pike's Peak, and loved Rocky Mountain National Park. But our favorite activity was learning to rock climb! We spent a few months climbing, kayaking, and enjoying fun, outdoorsy towns. Then we swung through Ohio for a quick visit and headed to Florida for the winter.

The first half of year eight revolved around Josh. Less than two months after his seventeenth birthday, he enlisted in the Marines. We stayed in Florida until he left for boot camp, and then circled the east coast so we could get back to Parris Island, South Carolina for his graduation thirteen weeks later. Since we were stuck in the east and missing Josh, we decided to repeat our amusement park theme. We hit Carowinds, Kings Dominion, and Dorney Park in Pennsylvania. We did sneak in a little rock climbing in Georgia at Currahee Mountain (from Band of Brothers)![3] Easy Company ran the mountain, saying "three miles up, three miles down". In June, Josh's graduation was incredible. We were so proud of him then (and still are now). We got to spend a fun week together until he left for his next training in North Carolina. (He's been stationed in Hawaii since then and has deployed to Okinawa once already. We still miss him!)

The second half of the year, we climbed. We were heading back to Colorado, when our friends, the Johnsons, convinced us to go to Oregon instead for the upcoming eclipse. So we joined them there, taught them to climb, and climbed together in Oregon, Washington, Utah, and Nevada. We headed to Florida in December and got to spend a few days with Josh who flew in for Christmas.

The theme of our ninth year seemed to be escaping Florida, and we spent half the year there. We stayed in one area so Lizzy could work and save money for a car. There were also driver permits, glasses, contacts, retreats, skin cancer surgeries, and other details that kept us longer. We missed traveling and especially climbing, but season passes to Disney helped. It was also a nice consolation when Allen, my brother, my mother, and I flew to visit Josh in Hawaii! In July, we finally escaped and went to Ohio to the annual softball tournament where Allen and I first met in 1996. His 2003 national champion team from Dailyville had a reunion and we had a blast. We saw so many of our friends and family, with many trips down Memory Lane. After that, we headed west to Colorado, and made it this time. We spent August climbing there and September hiking and canyoneering in Utah. Canyoneering is basically hiking with obstacles, so you may have to climb, rappel, shimmy, swim, or find a way around. Then we headed to Las Vegas for the winter, so we could climb, while Lizzy worked again.

We've begun our tenth year now and the theme is still undetermined. It may be empty nest, or will they ever leave the nest? Both Matt (seventeen) and Lizzy (nineteen) are currently working on their plans to launch. Matt is considering military and Lizzy is considering college and/or a job. Currently, we don't know their plans or our next location, but the unknown is pretty much our specialty. So for now, we'll just continue climbing and hiking in the beautiful mountains of Nevada. Then where will we go? Who knows? And that is our favorite place to go!

Now that Lizzy has a car, it's been convenient for quick trips without our giant truck. When we started, I didn't know how we would get along with only one vehicle. Three kids going in three different directions with two parent drivers can be challenging. What I didn't know was how different RV life would be. I didn't realize we would all simply go in the same direction, together. I didn't realize we wouldn't even go much at all. I wondered what would happen if Allen was gone with the truck and I needed to go somewhere. What I didn't know was our life would slow down so much and that "need" would go away. I never "need" to go anywhere. I can simply wait until Allen gets home. We have very few "needs" now.

We've made mistakes along the way, which we prefer to consider learning opportunities. And for nine years, we've had the opportunity to learn a lot. Many are hard to even consider mistakes though, because we've learned to simply be flexible and deal with things as they happen. Tires go flat, directions are wrong, and campgrounds are full, but since there is no schedule ruined, we just call it another adventure. But here are a few things we've learned the hard way.

Plan ahead when camping over holiday weekends. When you show up on a random Tuesday, campgrounds are usually quite empty. When you show up on the Fourth of July though, you better have reservations. We spent July 4, 2010 in a scary campground with a neighbor we called Loudy McYelly. It wasn't ideal, to say the least, but we still drove an hour to the ocean and saw a great fireworks show and the Blue Angels! There have been an embarrassing number of occasions when we've arrived not realizing it was a holiday weekend, spring break, etc. See the next paragraph to find out why we are so lame. When we start seeing people online, complaining or rejoicing about their kids being home from school soon, we now know to call ahead!

Be prepared not to know the time, day, or even month. We rarely know what day it is, as it usually doesn't matter. When many RVs start pulling in to the campgrounds, we realize it's Friday because the "weekenders" are here. Sometimes we'll first notice the TGIF posts on Facebook. We try to pay attention so we can attend a local church on Saturday or Sunday. We also try to avoid getting to campgrounds on Fridays because of the traffic. But there are still times we've gone to the post office to find it closed at 2pm on a Sunday, planned a day hike but realized it was almost dark, or worn shorts and forgot it was already winter there.

You can always find WiFi; it just might not be where you want it. As we work online and need internet access, this is a big deal. We generally stay at campgrounds with WiFi, and have a MiFi and smart phones, but even with these three options, we don't always have internet. When we first started out, we didn't know campground WiFi and cell service weren't always reliable. Sometimes we've gone without, but other times there were deadlines approaching and we've had to camp in less desirable areas with better signals. We figure it's our job, so we try not to complain. We've just learned not to depend on a signal being available and to be flexible if we have to move to find one or spend a few hours in town at a hotspot.

There will always be maintenance. Since our home is rolling around the country, the tires will blow and things will break. Of course that happens if you live in a house too! We don't have to pay utility bills, mow the lawn, pull weeds, plant flowers, paint the house, trim the bushes, or fix the fence, but we still budget for maintenance. That just includes tires and repairs now. We've been very fortunate and haven't needed very many repairs on our truck or RV. Sometimes it feels like we've changed way too many tires, but those tires have covered forty-eight states, pulling everything we own. In the beginning, we figured we'd need occasional maintenance, but we hadn't budgeted for it. Now we realize it's more of a "when" rather than an "if," so we budget for it and are prepared. Fortunately it's still much less than we spent maintaining our house and two vehicles!

There are challenges when hitting the road, including fear, reactions, money, resistance, and all the overwhelming details. But if your family is determined, you can make it happen. Once we decided, we were all so eager that nothing could stop us! It took a few months to sort out the details and do the manual labor of selling, buying, packing, and going. Some families plan for years, while others have managed it in just a few days. If your family is considering unlocating, you can do it! Nomadic life isn't for everyone, but if it's something you would love, we highly recommend it. Today is always the best day to start working toward your dream. And the trailblazer tribe will be very helpful.

Your dream doesn't have to look like ours, either. You don't have to unlocate permanently. You might save up and do an epic, three-month road trip and see as much as you can. Or you may choose to spend six months or a year traveling. You could carefully time a trip to happen right before a move to a new house, a new job, or a new state. You might find a short-term renter for your house, hit the road, and just see how long you enjoy it. You'd be surprised how many families we've met on the road who planned one-year trips, but haven't returned for many years because they loved the freedom so much. Then others have returned to their homes and lives, grateful for a trip full of memories.

Some people are very cautious in life. We are not those people. We've learned to try, fail, try again, start over, bomb, do it again, and nothing is final. So why not try things? If they don't work, try other things. We finally realized life is literally (not just figuratively) what you make it, and you can make it anything you want. So why not make it epic? We hear so many people say, "I can't do that," "I wish I could do that," and "You're so lucky." We are definitely not lucky. We're purposeful and determined and very blessed, yes. But we didn't hit any jackpot where we were handed this life. We worked hard to create it. So maybe we are lucky – lucky we're willing to work hard! I do believe God watches over us and has kept us alive, afloat, and redirected just when needed, so I don't think we get all the credit. But if you are waiting, you probably won't luck into an adventurous life. You have to go create it.

In case you incorrectly assume an amazing life is a perfect life, right now I'm listening to a seventeen-year-old complain about how boring his life is. Sadly, it is our seventeen-year-old. Our life is pretty amazing. We go to amazing places, learn about amazing things, and do amazing activities. This boy has spent his birthday at Mount Rushmore, Grand Canyon, Glacier National Park, Niagara Falls, and Worlds of Fun. But we also have plenty of normal times, when teenagers are bored. They have plenty of time to think their parents are mean, everyone else is having more fun, and life isn't fair. I don't know if that makes us awesome, horrible, or normal parents, but I'm sharing it in case you have teenagers. I just don't want you to think ours are always overly appreciative of our nomadic life, or pretty much anything else. Allen and

I can never fathom it, because we have the wisdom that comes with age I suppose. I'm confident as they look back over their life though, they'll remember more of the amazing and less of the boring. If you see them down the road, please feel free to remind them how lucky they are. It annoys them, which makes me smile.

Life on the road isn't always rosy, because life isn't always rosy. I assume no one's life is, as should you. Yes, we always see perfection displayed on social media, but that's because we share the best. Most of us have also hurriedly hidden things in closets before friends came to visit. Some people complain that isn't transparent enough. I personally think it's smart. It's social media, not confess your soul to strangers media. When I see your posed family pictures, I assume you have family fights on occasion. Looking at your pretty selfies, I assume sometimes you're a hot mess. I don't need to read about the fights or the messes. And you don't need to read about mine. Why would you want to? They're just like yours. If you simply want to feel assured that everyone else is as messed up as you, rest easy. We're all thumbing through our best photos, while fuming about something, trying to put our best foot forward. That's not fake. That's just saving our worst for a few close friends we trust. Sometimes my kids drive me crazy. Good grief, they're teenagers. Sometimes Allen drives me crazy. Listen, he's wonderful, but after twenty-two years, little things can become annoying. More often, I drive myself crazy. I feel bad for my family, who has to put up with me. But that's life, and it's not always rosy for anyone. What I love, though, is saying, "Hush up and buckle up, we're going to go see something amazing and you're going to like it."

So many people ask in real life, on social media, in messages, and by email, how they can become full-time RVers too. The trailblazer tribe is there to help. There are books, packing lists, videos, websites, Facebook groups, blogs, guides, clubs, and more. Some great resources are listed at the end of this book and on our website. Google will find millions more. You can learn about mobile income, mail forwarding, healthcare, roadschooling, maintenance, pets, and anything else you wonder about nomadic life.

We'd love to see you down the road! If you have no interest in un-locating, but you have a house with RV parking, we'd love to see you down the road too!

CHAPTER 3: UNSCHOOLING

As people learn that we live on the road full time, a common question is "Do you homeschool?" I always want to say, "We're not hauling a school around with us!" I usually resist, though. Yes, we live, work, play, and school, at home. Our home just happens to have wheels. Our homeschooling process, though, has changed greatly over the years. I have a feeling it will always be changing, as are the kids. It's hard to define and ever evolving, but the more we've reconsidered everything we knew about schooling, the better it seems to get.

We are roadschooling, which is simply learning on the road. We don't use a curriculum beyond life, because what a wide variety of topics life provides! As we travel, we learn together, about the area's history, customs, geography, attractions, culture, etc. We cover math, science, reading, and writing, by using them for daily life, not for a test. When the kids are curious about something, we research it together. So they learn the thing, how to find the thing, and that it's fun to find the thing! They're not in grades, or getting grades, but they're getting a solid education.

We're not traditionally homeschooling or recreating school at home. We did that for a while and, while it was easy to do in just a few hours each day, and the kids were grade levels ahead due to the individualized attention, it was still just the stressful memorization of facts someone else said were important. They would get it, then forget it, because that's what you do (that's what I did) when learning isn't a part of life. It was beneficial, and survivable, but not fun, for us or for the kids.

We are unschooling, which is simply learning without school. While some might assume unschooling means not schooling, which sounds like not learning, that's not even close. It just means learning without school. It's also called life learning, self-directed learning, independent learning, natural learning, child-led learning, delight driven learning, or autodidacticism. We live as if school didn't exist. Don't be appalled yet. Keep reading.

Our three kids learn very differently, so we help them dig into the way it works best for them. We're still learning. But just because our first son graduated at sixteen, aced the ASVAB, rocked the Marines at seventeen, and was accepted into college at eighteen, doesn't mean we are amazing parent-teachers. We just supported him as he did his thing. Josh knew his plan since Kindergarten and never changed it, only wavering between Army and Marines. We kept a paper he wrote for school, where he had to incorporate the five senses. Leaving the adorable six-year-old spelling, it said, "My favorite place to go is the army. I see mshene guns. I hear bullet fires. I smell smoke. I taste meet. I touch a grenade. The army is so panfull. By Josh Lundy."[4] And now we're supporting the other two as they're figuring out their things. It's awesome to help them and not feel we have to be the perfect un-schooling parents or the perfect homeschooling parents or pick the perfect school. Our kids are perfectly designed to learn and we love allowing that to happen naturally through unschooling.

It can be hard to define, but this is the best description I've found of unschooling:

"Think of school like a train ride from New York to LA. It has specific stops at specific times and will last a scheduled amount of time. Think of unschooling like crossing the country in an RV from NY to somewhere on the west coast. You won't be follow-ing the same route, won't be hitting the same cities. But you will be heading in the same general direction, following an interest-driven route." -Joyce Fetteroll.[5]

And it's not just the RV part that appeals to me, though it is fun. The learning still happens, just naturally through life.

There are so many learning opportunities on the road and every day is different. Sometimes we learn literally on the road, sitting in the truck, changing tires, or spotting wildlife out the windows. The Junior Ranger program[6] is a fabulous and fun way to learn about our national parks. The kids earn badges when they complete books from the parks and most are very challenging. Plus, national parks are just amazing places to see extraordinary things! The kids love to explore and try things out themselves. They especially love seeing, feeling, and touching history, so working farms ands mills with ancient equipment are intriguing. Of course location is always important. Learning about a fort, while sitting in that fort, is beyond cool and also hard to forget.

In our travels, we've been able to experience so many things firsthand, like military forts, battlefields, battleships, copper mines, Laura Ingalls Wilder sites, Charles Ingalls' actual fiddle, wagon wheel ruts from the Oregon Trail, backpacking in the country's only rainforest, the lowest spot in the country in Death Valley, the twelfth highest peak in Colorado on Mount Evans, forging metal with a blacksmith, running down the same runway the Wright brothers used for the first flight, seeing the actual plane they flew in Washington D.C., swimming with manatees, the actual Plymouth Rock, the Mayflower replica, and so many more. There are also a countless number of fascinating educational centers around the country, including science museums, aviation museums, history museums, nature centers, nature preserves, zoos, botanical gardens, aquariums, and imaginariums.

There is a wide range of unschooling philosophies and practices. I'm not going to tell you how unschooling should look in your family for two reasons. First, I'm not in your family. Secondly, I have no idea, because of the first reason. I will tell you how it looks in our family, though, and share some things we've learned over the years. Keep in mind we don't have a typical family. When you don't meet your kids until they are two, three, and six years old, the dynamic is very different from other families. Also we just don't like to be typical.

Another thing to keep in mind is I do know a bit about education. I'm just a few student-teaching hours short of an education degree. I went to a school. My parents were both teachers in schools. My grandmother, who also lived with us, was a teacher in a one-room school. That is why grammar was a big deal in our family, by the way. That is also why my brain almost melted when our second and third adopted kiddos came into our lives saying "ain't". Looking back now, that was hardly important, but to this schooled mama, it was rough. (I'm happy to report a solid few weeks of "ain't ain't a word and I ain't gonna say it" eliminated that word.) They were also Cleveland Browns fans and we were in southern Ohio, so obviously that was a problem too. (I'm happy to report they now correctly root for the Cincinnati Bengals, as hard as that is for all of us.)

Even Allen and I don't quite see eye to eye on unschooling. For example, I can let go of the "need for math". Yes, even though I have a degree in physics and mathematics, I don't think everyone needs to know all math. My husband, on the other hand, still has that common fear of "what if?" I'm not sure what that "what if" could ever amount to, though. Maybe China could invade the United States and randomly select citizens to complete algebra problems. Maybe a train station will lose power permanently and people will actually have to know how to work the infamous problem "Train A leaves Station One at 2:00pm traveling eighty miles per hour, while Train B leaves Station Two..." What I am sure of is our daughter's job will never require math. How do I know this? Because if her job ever did require math, she would quit and find a new job. Some jobs absolutely need math, engineering jobs for example. Our daughter will not be applying for those.

But what if they need it later? I know you're thinking it. It's simple though. They can learn it later. One unschooling family's son decided to go to college at eighteen. His mom told him he'd probably have to learn algebra, so he did. He bought a book, studied for a few months, and got into college. He didn't need to spend twelve years in math classes that built upon each other until he finally had enough knowledge. Now his degree will guide him through the math he will actually need for his life. (I realize that is debatable too, but that is another book for another day.)

There is certainly some math you will need in life, because you will use it in life. So why not learn it in life? I love how one of the trailblazers, Sandra Dodd, put it. "People will say 'How will they learn algebra in the real world?' Is there algebra in the real world? If not, why should it be learned? If so, why should it be separated artificially from its actual uses?"[7] So please don't think I'm anti-math. I love math actually. It's like me, black or white. Answers are either right or wrong. There is no subjectivity, gray area, or interpretation to argue about. It's also a part of life, so easily learned in life.

In full disclosure, I should share why we started homeschooling in the first place. It might surprise you. It sure surprised us. It wasn't on purpose. We never planned to homeschool. There are schools. Kids go to them. We simply never thought beyond that. We never thought, "We can do this!" We actually thought, "Oh crud, do we have to do this?" It's not a glorious story that shows how remarkable we are, but it's an interesting story that shows how we kind of had no choice.

The short version is we did "nothing" and it was better than school. Stick with me and I will explain with the long version. When Lizzy was eight, it was strongly suggested to us that it would be helpful to homeschool her for adoption-related reasons. We thought for about thirty seconds and refused. Keep in mind Matt would be entering Kindergarten, so all three kids would finally be in school all day. And since we worked from home, that was going to be wonderful. Five days a week of uninterrupted work time would certainly help our jobs. If you work at home and have little ones, I know you get me.

But with more nudging and suggesting it would really benefit Lizzy, we considered it more seriously. She did need time with just me because she never got that mom-time most kids get. She didn't have it in her past before us, or in her present, since she was in school all day and with her siblings all night. Still, we resisted. Both boys had time with just me to attach and do all the things moms and babies do naturally. Matt came to us at three and Josh was almost two, and they learned to love and trust doing those things. We finally stopped resisting and realized the suggestion was just right. Lizzy needed that time, so how could we not give it to her? We were still reluctant, but we decided to give her one year. Ideally, she just needed mom time, not education. Conveniently, she and Josh were in the same grade, so we could keep an eye on his homework and kind of gauge her progress. We figured we could help her catch up in the summer so she could return to school the next year. This unique position of having two children the same age turned out to be very helpful.

So in 2008, Lizzy started third grade at home, while the boys went to school. We went to the pool, went shopping, ran errands, rode bikes, cooked, baked, cleaned, read, played with dolls, played computer games, played inside, played outside, and played some more. That's it. All year.

And while she began the year far behind Josh, she ended it far ahead of him. What?! We were shocked too. We didn't teach. She didn't learn. But somehow we did, and she did, on accident.

Obviously, personal attention helped her self-esteem and confidence. Obviously, she picked up some math skills playing with the calculator in the grocery store. Obviously, she was absorbing history and science from her games and books. Obviously, we couldn't send her back to school. This is where we got really nervous. Obviously, if her year of "nothing" was better than their year of school, we couldn't send the boys back either. Matt was already showing signs that school would be challenging for him. More honestly, Matt would be challenging for the school. His wonderful Kindergarten teacher, bless his heart, had figured out Matt's learning style and attention limitations and made so many helpful allowances. We knew that wouldn't be possible every year though. But remember our dream of quiet work days? Ugh. So, while we planned to spend a year attaching, which was indeed effective, we accidentally spent a year learning.

Most people have lofty goals, plans, ideals, convictions, and strong feelings about why they want to homeschool. They planned and dreamed about this special time with their children. They couldn't wait to do it. We simply couldn't not do it after seeing the results of doing nothing, at home, together.

You might think less of me, knowing we fell into this instead of me being some super mom with a grand educational plan. But

I live by the idea that your opinion of me is none of my business, so that's okay. I am an amazing researcher though. And as I said, things are black and white for me. So when the evidence said it was more effective to have our kids at home, I believed it and dove into the world of homeschooling. My hypothesis was if Lizzy could learn this much without us teaching her, imagine what they could learn if we taught them a lot! What's funny is we've come full-circle and we now realize our first year with Lizzy was actually unschooling. But it took us a while to wrap our minds around it.

In our next year of homeschooling, we basically did school at home. We had a curriculum, Allen had his spreadsheets, and the kids had lessons. There were spelling tests, math worksheets, and music classes, but there were also cookie baking experiments, gym classes on the trampoline, and fun homeschool fieldtrips. It was easy to get a full day of school completed in just a few hours. Imagine a day at school without the administrative tasks, roll taking, announcements, bells, shuffling classes, passing out papers, spills, questions, repetitions, disruptions, corrections, and the many small things that come from having twenty or thirty kids in one room. So we were doing school, and it was effective by school standards, but I started noticing resistance. And it wasn't coming just from the kids. I could see them shifting around in boredom. I could hear them complaining about having to do certain classes. But I could feel them worrying that homeschool was simply going to be school at home. And I was worrying about that too.

I admit I started to resist the structured learning, possibly more than the kids. Allen, the business guy who thrives in a routine, taught his chosen subjects at his appointed times on his infernal spreadsheets. It's not surprising he chose the three R's, reading, writing, and arithmetic. He had to cover those basics – just in case. As for me, though I love math and the black and white rules, I also crave freedom and artistic expression. So my teaching time was a bit more relaxed. I taught from a curriculum which used the Little House on the Prairie books. We would read a chapter and then do a few activities from different subjects mentioned in our reading. It covered areas such as math, science, history, literature, nutrition, Bible, vocabulary, reading, music, art, logic, character, cooking, and health. When Laura wondered about the moon, we studied it. When they discussed blood cells, we watched blood component videos on YouTube. I preferred the more fun activities though. When the Ingalls family talked about the California gold rush, we had a gold rush, searching for a golden egg filled with candy. When they mentioned oats, we made honey oat bread. I think the more structured Allen was, the more I resisted. My research was also leading me toward unschooling, which of course Allen resisted. He thought it sounded irresponsible, lazy, weird, and worst of all, it wouldn't fit into a spreadsheet.

As a good wife, I didn't listen. We compromised with "You do it your way and I'll do it mine." I started finding the trailblazers and learning all I could. As a researcher, I gathered my data. I studied our guinea pigs, I mean children. I watched how they learned. I also watched Allen learn, because I knew he'd get it eventually.

As I started assigning less, we were finding them doing more on their own. Josh was very self-motivated and loved to learn. He watched the military and history channels, no cartoons for him. One day Lizzy and Matt measured the circumference of every tree in the yard (and there were a lot!) to find the oldest. They learned about that on a cereal box. When I stopped officially teaching from the Little House curriculum, they begged me to read chapter after chapter (and still learned the history, science, literature, Bible, character, etc. - without realizing it). Matt continued with his math workbook because he wanted to catch Josh and Lizzy. Lizzy kept creating wonderful art projects just for fun. She recreated the Phoenix landing on Mars after seeing it on TV. Matt helped Allen fix the belt on the lawn mower. Josh continually spewed facts from documentaries, books, and videos. So they learned and Allen learned. He really came to understand unschooling, which was worth the wait.

When he agreed to give it a real chance, he was still hesitant but I assured him nothing was final. They could always go back to school. I said we could make them take a class every few years to be sure they could catch up. And we tried it. The Great Math Experiment confirmed my theory. After years of no math, we put them in online classes at their typical grade levels. They did well, with very minimal effort. It was tiring though, proving their knowledge with assignments and tests, and even proving our parental involvement with required calls and emails. Lizzy said, "Mom, you couldn't be more involved, we live in forty feet." Of course it's actually four hundred square feet. Remember, she avoids math. So, no more classes. We went back to just learning for fun.

When they watched TV shows like Duck Dynasty, Pawn Stars, or I Shouldn't Be Alive, they learned new things. Josh would say some box is from some war because of some fact he saw in some pawn shop. They climbed trees to cut mistletoe, which we learned grows in bird poo, to sell in campgrounds. Of course they watched us like hawks too, learning about whatever we were doing. Refinishing tables, remodeling, truck maintenance, hunting safety, fantasy football, running a business, grocery budgeting, cooking, complaining about (but always paying) taxes, etc. They're never far (literally, we live in a box), so we're always learning from each other.

Some of their favorite areas of study were aerodynamics and physics, specifically trajectory and inertia, physical fitness, and a bit of first aid. Yes, the trampoline was our most-loved educational tool. They spent hours on that thing having fun. I've heard quite a few people say, "Life isn't fun, so school shouldn't be fun." That is just so sad and frankly, their life must stink! Our life is super fun and we certainly wanted learning to be fun too.

Josh asked to study "the effects of the sun on my skin as I play outside and get tan." I agreed, as long as he could tell me why the skin's color changes. He grumbled but was actually intrigued. Matt guessed it was like how a toaster toasts bread. But if I would have sat them down for a health class and taught about melanin pigment, they would have been bored. They might have memorized it for a test even, but it would mean little, if anything, later on. This way, they were interested and wanted to understand how it worked.

My iPhone battery completely died and instead of paying to replace the battery, I bought a new phone. I watched a video on how to replace it yourself and it looked way over my head. Josh wanted to try and I said he could have mine if he fixed it. He spent $8 on parts and a lot of time learning about the insides of iPhones and got a new phone!

Once we hit the road, the learning opportunities were endless. We were always going to fascinating new places and learning about history, geography, geology, science, culture, food, etc. It's actually impossible not to unschool as you explore, whether you realize it's happening or not. While our Little House curriculum was fun and all-encompassing, we did something even better. We visited all of the places from the books and saw exactly where Laura Ingalls lived! We camped on the bank of Plum Creek and visited their original homestead claim. We saw so many pieces of history, including the site of their dugout, the actual Cottonwood trees Pa planted, Lake Pepin, Silver Lake, the twin lakes, the Oleson Mercantile site (though the original building burned down in the early 1900s), the bell Pa helped to buy, his actual fiddle, Laura's treasured china, the house where she wrote the books, and the graves of most of the family, Mr. Boast, and Reverend Brown.

Because we're always watching for learning opportunities, we accidentally found a fabulous, free zoo in Pennsylvania. Driving by the Nemacolin Resort, we saw a sign that read "Enter at Own Risk," so naturally we stopped to investigate since that sounded intriguing. We found extremely friendly animals, with just a small gate between us! The camels, llamas, sheep, and goats loved attention. Beyond that area, there were many other wild animals in natural habitats, including bighorn sheep, bears, lions, buffalo, and zebras. And all of this was free, open to visitors, with hardly anyone around, no lines, and no traffic. It was such a cool encounter.

One of our absolute favorite hands-on educational experiences of the past nine years was watching the neon blue waves in the ocean near San Diego! Allen heard about the bioluminescent phytoplankton (red tide by day, blue waves by night). We wanted to go check it out, but we weren't sure if we would actually find it. So we drove by the Pacific Ocean as the sun went down, hoping. And WOW! All of a sudden, looking out the windows, we could see the tops of the ocean waves light up with electric blue. It was absolutely amazing! We parked, hit the beach, and watched for hours. It was seriously one of the most fascinating things we've seen in our lives. And it was so pretty. Wave after wave would start glowing, then building, then crashing, with the blue color getting brighter and brighter. As it got darker, the color of the waves intensified. We dug in the sand and it glowed beneath our fingers. The kids ran and splashed and fell and glowed and had a great time. We filled a jar with water too and it glowed when we shook it. So we got to take it home to enjoy a little longer. Don't worry, this is different from the algal blooms they call red tide in Florida, and aren't toxic. Of course we did that research!

We may have learned the most during our RVsteading adventures in Arkansas. As I shared in the unlocating chapter, we raised, grew, or hunted for our food. We had to understand animal care, breeding, birthing, and processing. We learned about gardening, foraging, cooking, and canning. And we were always building, clearing, shaping, and improving the land. It was fascinating to see how much goes into providing your own needs. And we just scratched the surface too. We're definitely grateful for that education and for the tribe who helped us along the way.

Since we don't "do school", you might be surprised at our excitement about an online class we took. "We" meaning "I forced the kids do it because I wanted them to and I knew Allen and I would like it too." And we were all very pleasantly surprised! It was based on The Hunger Games, so I knew I had Lizzy's attention. It was called On Tyrants & Tributes- Real World Lessons From The Hunger Games.[8] It was a free week-long class by LearnLiberty.org, with videos, discussion questions, points to earn, and a live chat at the end. It covered the history and mythology which inspired the book. They were great lessons for the kids, who hadn't been interested in such things before. They discussed past and present political issues in the book. It was so interesting! I knew the kids would benefit from it, but I learned so much myself. The kids loved the books and movies, and we even went to a filming location. So I knew it had the potential to keep their attention, but the quality and quantity of information in this class far exceeded my expectations. While our kids were fourteen, fourteen, and eleven, the other students were college-age and older. This is really a great resource for homeschooling, roadschooling, and yes, even unschooling!

But what about socialization? You might be thinking it. I can't believe this question is still asked about homeschoolers, but it is. Frequently. Before quality of education even. "What about socialization? Kids need to go to school to learn socialization."

First, the definition of socialization (noun) is "a continuing process whereby an individual acquires a personal identity and learns the norms, values, behavior, and social skills appropriate to his or her social position."[9] No, we don't want that from school. Now, maybe they mean will they be socialized (verb) which means "to make social; make fit for life in companionship with others"?[10] Yes, they will. It really is that easy. There are many books, articles, and blog posts that share the ways homeschoolers are involved with a wide variety of group activities. I would ask my kids for input, but they're off socializing. Go ask our friend Google. It's been proven countless ways homeschoolers manage just fine in the real world. Yet the question continues.

But how can socialization at school be the answer when there's no other time in life where you are surrounded by peers of only your own age? At your job, you will compete with older people with more experience and younger people with more education. You will collaborate with people with vastly different interests, backgrounds, values, morals, religions, etc., most of which aren't very different in classrooms. Where can kids prepare for this then? At pretty much every activity outside of school. So my kids are fine. Your kids are fine. You can take socialization off of your "to worry about" list.

But how will you know if they're learning what they need to learn? If you are there, you will know. Unlike school, where they attempt to measure learning, you will know. You will see it, experience it, and be a part of it. If you had thirty kids in a classroom, you may need other options. But if you only have two, five, or ten kids, you will know. You will see if they're good at important, relevant things they will need in life. You won't have to test their knowledge, because you will watch them use it. They won't miss the chance at jobs, careers, or colleges, because you will help them prepare for those.

No teacher, not even the world's most talented, captivating, and amazing teacher, could love your children more than you. So no one could be better than you to help your children prepare for life. Do you feel incapable of teaching your children? Should you send them to a school that left you feeling incapable of teaching your children? Give that some thought before you send the email. I'm just asking questions, not telling you what to do.

Some worry that homeschoolers and especially unschoolers aren't properly tested, like they would be at school. But I would argue that the testing at school isn't really hitting the mark either. I love what Seth Godin wrote, "The essential thing measured by school is whether or not you are good at school. Being good at school is a fine skill if you intend to do school forever. For the rest of us, being good at school is a little like being good at Frisbee. It's nice, but it's not relevant unless your career involves homework assignments, looking through textbooks for answers that are already known to your supervisors, complying with instructions, and then, in high-pressure settings, regurgitating those facts with little processing on your part."[11] And since most careers aren't like that at all, I'm grateful we can help our children skip school and prepare for real life, while living in the real life. Sandra Dodd, said it this way, "Kids who are in school just visit life sometimes, and then they have to stop to do homework or go to sleep early or get to school on time. They're constantly reminded they are preparing 'for real life,' while being isolated from it."[12]

In case you're wondering, yes, unschooling is legal in all fifty states. Each state has separate requirements for homeschoolers from none at all to periodic testing. Just find the unschooling groups in your state and they will assist you with those details. There are so many options like notices, umbrella schools, calendars, portfolios, and teacher reviews, and your local tribe will be happy to help. Of course if you are unlocating, choosing a state with few regulations as your state of residency is a great perk.

You might already embrace unschooling, but have family or friends who are giving you a hard time. We certainly did. Remember my teacher parents? They were worried, but now they're our biggest fans. Keep in mind they love you. They're just afraid, because they don't understand it. You and I both might have done the same thing before we learned more. Just be sure to watch for the trailblazers who can help, instead of only listening to the naysayers. While your loved ones truly mean well, the trailblazer tribe will support you. Joyce Fetteroll said it this way. "What you're dealing with is a very well-meaning person who is convinced the world is flat and is worried that you're so clueless that you want to head off across the horizon. It's a lot healthier and more useful to listen to the people who've been across the horizon than to the person who fears it."[13]

You also might worry about what I think, if you don't choose to unschool, roadschool, or homeschool. I don't know why you would care what I think, but let me reassure you. I have three children and they consume 100% of my mental capacity. I am responsible for their health and well being, including their education and preparation for the future. Like most parents, I'm pretty sure I'm screwing it up. But that is my job and I take it very seriously. And it is exhausting. I promise you I have never, and will never, spend one minute worrying about how you raise or educate your own children. It's not because I don't care about them, or you. I simply don't have the mental energy for it. So please don't ever worry about my opinion. My only opinion of you is, if you're a parent, I'm sure you will do the absolute best for your children, no matter what it looks like. And whatever path you take, I know you will find your tribe to help.

Amy Dingmann summed it up perfectly. "There is no award for the homeschooliest homeschooler or the unschooliest unschooler. So maybe just concentrate on whatever glorious mix of life and learning works for your family."[14] I love this so much! Some of our kids embraced unschooling so well and some were, let's just say more challenging. We've had such a mix of education around here. If it were just me, I would totally do things a certain way. But since it's them, and they're so not me (thank goodness, right?!), I'm just happy we have the freedom to help them dig into learning the way it works best for them.

In attempting to teach our children, we've learned a lot ourselves. In our homeschooling adventures, we've run the gamut of keeping up with our local school to pushing them to be grades ahead to allowing them to be grades behind to realizing none of that matters. We simply want them to love to learn, so we simply love to learn along with them.

I wish more parents realized they could spend every day with their kids, preparing them well for life, while enjoying their time together.
•Imagine our wealthy friends teaching their kids successful entrepreneurship.
Imagine our struggling friends teaching their kids to overcome.
•Imagine our friends who've always wanted to travel teaching their kids on the road.
•Imagine our friends who don't travel teaching their kids to appreciate their hometown roots.
•Imagine our world with families who spend their days together, parents who are fully present, and children who learn alongside those who love them most.

According to John Taylor Gatto, "There isn't a right way to become educated; there are as many ways as there are fingerprints."[15] This is so true. Our three kids all learn very differently. The beauty of unschooling, for our family, is that they're free to and we're free to do it right along with them.

Margie Lundy

CHAPTER 4: UNWORKING

Another common question people ask, when they find out we are nomads, is what we do for a living. We're often met with confusion at campgrounds, because we're not old enough to be retired and we don't look like we're on vacation. Since the majority of campgrounds are full of retirees, with families only camping on weekends or vacations, we are a bit of an oddity. If only they knew how odd! But we actually love that question, because we get to share how we help people change their lives and how much we enjoy it. That itself is an oddity in a campground with retirees who finally escaped their jobs or vacationing families trying to get away from theirs.

So yes, we work from our home, which has wheels. Just like our life, our career is completely mobile. We have two offices with laptops and a printer, though we honestly do most of our work on our phones. We have mentors, partners, and clients all over the country and we stay connected online. We utilize video chats, calls, texts, messages, emails, and groups to keep in touch. And we rely on ridiculous animated GIFs to express emotion. We also love meeting in person, which is a huge perk of our traveling life.

We are working, just not traditionally. In undoing what we thought about working, we began unworking. Yes, it's quite common among RVers, since our lives are untraditional. Many trailblazers are out there rethinking traditional jobs. There are numerous books, websites, and podcasts to help you learn about remote work, seasonal jobs, entrepreneurship, multiple income streams, and more.

Allen and I do work together and we have since 2004. Of course that might sound either romantic or horrific, depending on your personal perspective. We find it to be a little of both. The main thing we've learned in working together is we do not work together. That might sound contradictory, but it took us many years to come to understand this truth. We work very well, side by side, using our individual strengths. We have so much trust and respect for each other's areas of expertise and we've learned to work from those. We've also learned not to expect each other to work the way we do. So Allen looks at the big picture and he doesn't expect me to pay much attention to the grand plan. I focus on the details and I don't expect him to notice all the small tasks that make the plan come together. He connects with people and I connect the dots.

Maybe you have a smooth, symbiotic working relationship with your spouse, where you read each other's minds and never argue. If so, I should be reading your book, so please get started. Maybe yours isn't as smooth, but you're working out a good system together. Hang in there, it's worth it. Maybe yours is less than ideal and you've agreed never to work together. Maybe you don't have a spouse. Fortunately, you don't have to. There is such a wide variety of jobs, both online and offline, that you can find the perfect fit for you.

Some jobs are perfect for a technology minded individual, such as computer programming, website design, virtual assisting, or video editing. A more artistic person might prefer jewelry making, painting, music, or graphic design. An extrovert might teach a class or tutor students. An introvert might be a writer or a transcriptionist. If you love sales and helping others, you might sell skin care or cookware. If you don't, you may like housesitting or petsitting.

If you'd prefer a team approach, searching for bargains to resell online could be fun. Partners can be very helpful for content creators, podcasters, travel agents, and social media managers. Doing product reviews, instructional videos, or travel blogging is much easier for two. Of course you could work with your spouse, your child, a relative, a friend, or even a stranger you meet online.

You might even want to take a family approach and run a business with everyone's help. Unschooling? Check! What better way is there of teaching your children to succeed in business than helping them succeed in business? They might learn to source products, post on social media, keep the books, do sales presentations, make phone calls, create graphics, edit videos, write blog posts, and so much more. You can lighten your load, while strengthening their portfolios. Unworking could be a huge head start for their lives.

Some jobs are location based, like helping with a seasonal harvest, working for an Amazon fulfillment center, or working at an amusement park. Some jobs are travel based, like driving trucks, working at festivals, or working on cruise ships. Some jobs require travel, but then are locally based for the duration of the job, like travel nursing, construction, or pipelines. Many campgrounds will offer a free campsite and sometimes hourly pay, in exchange for work such as hosting, registration, maintenance, or cleaning.

While those jobs don't appeal to us, because we like our freedom, they work perfectly for others. Some people like to stay put for months, to have time to fully explore each area. Others like to work really hard for a season, and then not have to work at all for the rest of the year. Some enjoy seeing what they can as they travel, while having the comfort and security of consistent jobs and paychecks. We've met hundreds of travelers with hundreds of different types of jobs. It's amazing to see the variety and great to know there is something for everyone. And according to Darren Hardy, the top ten most sought-after jobs today did not even exist ten years ago.[16] So you might have to wait on your ideal job. Or you might have to invent it! I've shared many mobile income ideas, but you can find more on our website (www.tinyurl.com/how2rv) and in the resources at the end of this book.

Allen and I prefer completely mobile jobs, so we are free to move about the country at will. As transformation coaches, we get to help people change their whole lives, including their physical, mental, and financial health. While we're becoming the best versions of ourselves, we help others become the best version of themselves. It's encouraging, because we get to hear how our friends are doing on their health journeys or with their new businesses. We are surrounded each day by people who are striving to improve every area of their lives. That is a wonderfully positive work environment!

We wake up to messages about people getting off medications, picking up hobbies, or paying off debt. Their health goals range from toning up to losing significant amounts of weight to making life-saving changes. Business goals range from making a little extra money for special activities to replacing incomes to leaving legacies. It's so inspiring to see a client change her goal from something small she really didn't think was possible, to something huge she knows she can accomplish. It's wonderful to see healthy changes affect entire families too. It's gratifying to be a part of changing not only lives, but family trees!

While it is by far the most rewarding career we've ever had, it also pays very well. We like to say we get paid well for doing good. We earn full-time pay, without full-time hours, just for helping others. We coach clients in using nutrition to get healthy and reach their goals. We help partners strengthen their relationships and increase their community involvement. We mentor coaches who are building strong businesses and finding freedom.

We don't have long, hard work days, but we do work hard, for a few hours a day. And those hours are usually designed around a day of adventure, because we like helping people and we like having fun! Since we do most of our work on our phones, we can be anywhere and still be available. We can answer questions, check in with clients, and follow up with coaches no matter where we are. We schedule calls before or after hiking or climbing. Or sometimes we'll just pause to rest, take a call, then continue with the hike or climb. If we need to prepare for an important training or be available all day to a new coach, we just climb the following day. Since every day is wide open, we don't have to rush to get things in. The next chapter explains how we keep our schedule clear.

Even though we are very relaxed around here, Allen and I work hard on self development and leadership skills. We have structured work time when needed. We just don't need it as often as busier people. If, like me, you love books on leadership that get you motivated and excited to reach goals, just know this one is quite a bit different. Hopefully it will still get you pumped for your goals, but I won't be sharing daily lists, routines, characteristics, methods, practices, and the like. Those are out there and I recommend them. But our leadership style is a little more chill. We're more about if you have a goal, figure out how to get it, and start getting it. We tend to simplify things and just go for it. It may take us two years to save for a truck, but we don't have a two-year plan with eighteen steps and daily tasks to track. So if this book feels a little oversimplified, it's just because our life actually is.

Despite what we've heard from so many people who call us "lucky", we weren't simply blessed with a career that gave us complete location, time, and financial freedom. No one handed us a job that included happy clients, encouraging partners, and hefty paychecks. Listen, I would have stood in a line for days for that! We had to decide, work, learn, grow, fail, learn some more, fail some more, and then succeed. But we had great mentors all along the way. We still do! Now we are blessed to be able to share that with others. We can't hand you those clients, partners, and paychecks either, so don't get in line with your tent and snacks. We do, though, love mentoring others on their own journeys of learning and succeeding.

We've had a few different sources of income since we hit the road in 2010. We owned an online graphics company, ran an online store with drop shipping, and did some remote bookkeeping. We've also had rental income and some investments. While none of those compare to our income for the past few years, a great thing about RVing is that it doesn't have to be very expensive. Of course "expensive" is relative and varies widely. If you polled one hundred RVing families about their monthly budget, you would get one hundred different answers, ranging from $1,000 a month to $10,000 a month. We've heard that discussion so many times over the years and it's quite funny. Those on the lower end can't fathom spending as much each month as those on the higher end.

And those on the higher end can't imagine how those on the lower end are scraping by. For a quick frame of reference, think of your income. Then think of your life without a mortgage, car payments, utility bills, lawn care, home owner association fees, or property taxes.

We lived on a pretty meager income during our first few years of travel, though we always had more than enough. Of course the kids had no idea and we were having a blast exploring the country. I'll never forget the day Matt learned of our actual income. He'd fallen at the campground and we suspected a broken collarbone, so we headed to the local hospital. Since we were paying with cash, I had to answer some questions for his forms. Though I tried to whisper, he overheard our income for the year. He asked if that number was a lot or not and I said it was plenty. The clerk handed me an informational sheet and he saw that our number was below the poverty line. He asked, "Doesn't poverty mean poor? Are we poor?!" I told him the government thought so, but they didn't know how amazing our life was. He went home, his arm in a sling for the broken bone, and asked Allen if he knew we were poor! We've had seasons of want and seasons of plenty, but our life hasn't changed very drastically, because we've already found freedom.

We're making six times more than that now, but life is still much the same. It's the same amazing life we've always enjoyed. When you can go wherever and do whatever, whenever, that's a life of freedom. And we have that because we've undone everything we thought. We've had that while making a little and we've had that while making a lot. Of course it's quite nice making a lot! That means we're able to give more, invest more, plan more, and check our bank accounts less.

We didn't even start this job on purpose. Allen and I ran into our friends, the Johnson family, who I mentioned in the unlocating chapter. We'd known them online for many years, but finally met at a gathering in Texas. Although we had seen them struggle with their weight, now they were so healthy, happy, energetic, and excited. And we wanted that! As they helped us get healthy, we knew our friends, and now our coaches, were doing something special. They loved it, helped so many people, and got paid well. Their job was about changing lives in amazing ways. And we wanted that too!

Allen and I hit our goals and were both at our high school weights, something we didn't realize was even possible. Best of all, we are still at those same weights over three years later, thanks to our new healthy habits and to the accountability of coaching. We learned more about coaching and our friends, and now our mentors, helped us along the way. We have an awesome team coaching model that simply, and powerfully, helps more people to help more people. Since we like stepping into the unknown, we were very open to trying something new. We decided to give it one month. What did we have to lose?

Well, in that month, we fell in love with coaching. In the following month, we replaced our income! While we loved the health aspects of losing weight, feeling better, and being more pleasant and present for our kids, we really loved the business aspects of helping others gain this freedom too. It's a more rewarding job than we've ever had. It keeps us accountable because we know so many are depending on us. And it pays very well.

Our health journey quickly became about so much more than just healthy bodies. Healthy minds and healthy finances are equally as important and we love that our coaching includes all three. We've expanded even further, utilizing our many years of experience, on and off the road, to teach freedom of the areas in this book. We believe mastery of these areas is where true freedom is found and we love sharing that with others.

A really fun part about our job is that it doesn't feel like a job at all. We don't have to sell, present, demonstrate, mail, or display anything. We just go about our adventurous life and talk to friends, old and new. We're certainly grateful for our healthy bodies, minds, and finances and it shows. We may be rock climbing, enjoying a local festival, or going out for sushi, but we're also working. We may be connecting with people, helping others reach for their goals, or showing what's possible, but we're also playing. People know we help transform lives in those areas. Sometimes they ask us to help, sometimes they don't. We're happy to help when we're needed, and happy when we're not. Because we're not worried about income, we don't have to put in more and more hours. But because we love helping others not have to worry about income, we love putting in the hours we do. This quote by L.P. Jacks sums us up perfectly. "A master in the art of living draws no sharp distinction between his work and his play; his labor and his leisure; his mind and his body; his education and his recreation. He hardly knows which is which. He simply pursues his vision of excellence through whatever he is doing, and leaves others to determine whether he is working or playing. To himself, he always appears to be doing both."[17]

Because we so easily integrate our job into our life, and our life is full of freedom, I've noticed some interesting nuances between nomads and house livers. I've seen this in our job and other industries as well. Sometimes certain training or advice doesn't easily apply to RVers. In the next chapter about unscheduling, you'll learn why we don't need to manage busy calendars or incorporate time blocking. We also don't have to try very hard to meet new people, because each time we move to the next campground, we have a brand new neighborhood full of potential friends. Trainers often like to use this quote to motivate: "Don't be afraid to give up the good to go for the great."[18] People usually nod in agreement and start looking for areas to sacrifice. This may not be popular, not that I have ever cared about that obviously, but that one just rubs me wrong. Because it's so widely accepted, I tried to embrace it, but I just couldn't. It took me a while, but I was able to pinpoint my problem with it. We already have the freedom most people are working toward.

We already have the great. And we don't have to give up any good to get more of the great. We could have a lot more great, obviously. This could bring more income, more influence, more prestige, more generosity, more compassion, and even more freedom. We could do more, be more, and help more. And that is absolutely our plan. But we don't have to give up time with our family. We're already together twenty-four hours a day, seven days a week. Our teenagers tell us that is way too much time some days! We don't have to hire help for household jobs, because we have so few of those. We don't have to give up activities to make time for work, because our days are wide open. We have already shed most of the extras many are learning to let go of.

We don't have the typical busy lives, so we don't need to make more time to work. I mentioned that we work a few hours a day. That's really more admitting than bragging, because we certainly could do more. We could literally work twice as hard every day, and that still wouldn't be full-time hours. But it's also important to us to leave a lot of time to play, especially with our children. They will only be with us for a little while longer. So it just doesn't make a lot of sense to give up freedom now, to work really hard, to get freedom later. And when you can do anything, anywhere, anytime, that is complete freedom. Of course we will always be working to have more freedom, and more importantly, to help others find that freedom. But we don't have to give up anything to do that.

Maybe you don't have that freedom yet, but you're interested. If you're still trying to build your income, but you want to travel, there are many ways of reducing expenses. Like I mentioned earlier, some campgrounds will offer free sites in exchange for hours of labor. If you're willing to work while camping, this is often called workamping. You can check with private campgrounds, state parks, or national parks or search for workamping opportunities online. Just keep in mind, depending on the value of the site and the hours required, sometimes it would make more financial sense to find a temporary local job and pay for the site. Or maybe you can workamp to lower your expenses, while your spouse works online or locally to increase your income.

You can even camp for free on public land, if you're willing to go without the conveniences. This is called boondocking. Many people love being off the grid like this and do it full time. We are not those people. We like water, electric, and sewer hookups, plus hot tubs, laundry rooms, and gyms at the campgrounds. We do like to occasionally boondock for a week or two though, just to get unplugged and away from the crowds. But if boondocking sounds amazing to you, there are many resources to help you get started. There's an established tribe of trailblazers too, so you can learn all about public land, solar power, or composting commodes. I'll share more about our boondocking adventures in the unplugging chapter.

Besides the cost of camping, it would be helpful if you could reduce your current expenses. Tracking where your money goes and sticking to a budget is important. If you don't do that yet, I suggest you trim as many expenses as you can first, and then get to work on tracking and budgeting. Maybe you're ready to ditch cable, since you Netflix anyway. Maybe you can let go of the gym membership you don't use, which then makes you feel guilty. Maybe you could skip eating out a few times a week, stop buying coffee on the way home, or cancel that magazine subscription you don't often read. Look at your bills and see what you could let go of. You might be surprised. There are lots of books and articles about cutting your expenses if you need more help.

Once you're ready to start budgeting and saving for the future, I recommend you read Dave Ramsey's Seven Baby Steps.[19] Those are the steps we used years ago to become debt free. If you can start working toward your dream of freedom, without bringing debt, the income part will be much easier. Whether your freedom means an RVing life, international travel, a dream home, or a backyard pool, beginning without debt would really help. It's not a deal breaker, though, especially if you have a good source of income.

There are so many resources about saving money and reducing your expenses, both in the real world and in the RV world. And yes, those are two very different worlds. For example, RVers can't easily shop in bulk to save money, because kitchen and storage space is limited. And we can't use loyalty card rewards if we're not in one area very long. It's also hard to use coupons if we're not sure which stores are near our next location. But there are many strategies available and of course the trailblazers will help. There are groups about things like saving money on groceries, free family entertainment, and low cost roadschooling activities.

One of my favorite resources is MoneySavingMom.com[20]. There you can learn about saving on groceries, with store-specific sales, restaurant deals, and coupon information. Plus, you'll find many other deals, giveaways, and freebies. She also shares about freezer cooking, menu planning, and recipes. Beyond saving money, she also provides money management and income earning ideas, and offers courses and books about blogging, productivity, and online income. And her stories on Instagram crack me up! Look for those trailblazers, though. They're out there waiting to help, if you're ready to consider unworking.

No matter our income, Allen and I have always been frugal for sport. We'll spend hundreds on something fun, but then haggle over a few pennies. We always choose the least expensive option, unless that's too restrictive. It's not really definable or easy to explain, but it's just how we operate. We'll go on a spontaneous cruise, but we won't buy pop from a drive-through. That's soda if you're not from the Midwest, or Coke if you're from the south. We were once going to a movie with a friend and I checked the show times. I said we could go at 11:00am. She asked if there weren't later times available. Of course there were, but it hadn't even crossed my mind to not choose the lower priced matinee. She asked if we needed extra cash and we just laughed. It's not about the need, it's just what we do, usually. If that movie would have been much better in 3-D, though, we'd gladly have paid the higher price.

One of our children's friends once called us "the cheapest rich people" she knew. I actually love that! It describes us pretty well and I think Dave Ramsey would be proud. Whether we were making a lot or a little, and we've had some crazy ups and downs, we've always been budget minded. And that's allowed us to always have plenty. Usually in this country, expenditures rise to meet income. We've worked really hard to avoid that. It's not an RVing cautious life thing though; it's just another example of our family not being very traditional.

Those were our practices before RVing, and they haven't changed. If you decide to hit the road, yours likely won't either. You could be thrifty and conscientious or you could be extravagant and lavish, but you would probably be however you are right now. If you tend to overspend your budget each month in a house, you will likely overspend on the road. If you rock at stretching your dollars in a house, you will probably do the same on the road. It's not like a monthly budget for a family of five in a house ranges from $3,000 to $12,000, but on the road it is exactly $4,128. You will see the same ranges, because people have the same tendencies. You can't decide if you will save money on the road, or need some extra income, without knowing exactly how your money is spent. Of course it's possible for you to change your habits and decrease your expenses, with purpose and intention.

If you aren't sure if you would be making enough for your dream, you could always try it out at home. If you know what you would make with an online job, try living off of only that for a few months. Put all of the rest automatically into savings and see how it goes with the smaller paycheck. Look at the bills you will no longer have, like a mortgage, electric, water, sewer, trash, lawn care, cable, etc. Next, look at the ones you will add, such as RV payments, fuel, camping, airfare, hotels, etc. A quick search online will find many budget examples to help you estimate these new costs. Then look at the amount you'll need to live on after those bills. This will be similar to what you need now. You will still need groceries, supplies, clothing, insurance, healthcare, entertainment, etc. Once you have a clear picture of your spending needs, you will know if you should work on increasing your income, decreasing your expenses, doing both, or immediately striking out without fear!

So if you have a big dream your current income doesn't allow you to move toward, maybe it's time to undo what you think about your job. Is working hard enough to just pay your bills really working for you? Or is it just working for your boss? Could you benefit from unworking? Of course no one's making you reach for your dreams. I'm just asking questions. Many feel like they should give up their dreams to better provide for their family, so their children can reach for their dreams. But often, those children just grow up thinking the best way to live is to give up their dream for their children, and the cycle continues. What if you teach your children to reach for their dreams by reaching for yours? You certainly don't have to sacrifice your kids' futures; please don't do that. But if you rethink work, maybe you can devise a plan which benefits the entire family. Or plan to achieve your freedom when the kids are older or when they leave the nest. Whatever freedom you desire, unworking can help you get it.

CHAPTER 5: UNSCHEDULING

This is going to be a tricky chapter, because you are probably very proud of your over-filled schedule. You're also exhausted and stressed out, but don't worry. You can keep your calendar color-coded, time-blocked, and maxed out. You can keep your "I'm so busy" badge that feels really good to wear. If you're happy with your calendar, that is wonderful. But I suggest you consider if your calendar is really benefiting your family or just keeping them busy. If you love it, read on for the stories and ignore any advice. If you don't, just read on.

I've often read the phrase, "busy is the new fine" and sadly, this has been true for many years now. It appeared in blog posts as early as 2011 and also in the 2010 book, The Power of Slow.[21] So the world has been proud of "busy" for a long time. Before then, we all knew "fine" meant "good", "okay", or "bad, but I'm not going to admit that to you." Today, we know "busy" means "important", "see how much I love my family or job", or "I'm overwhelmed, but don't know how to fix it." Another phrase, "stop the glorification of busy," started appearing on blogs around 2012, though no one seems to know who said it first. No matter who it was, I totally agree! I find it interesting that soon after this busy trend started getting noticed, there were trailblazers fighting against it.

Maybe you'll set aside your "I'm so busy" badge for just a moment and open your mind to clearing your schedule. At least a little? Maybe you're not ready, but you are reading a book about finding freedom. You would be amazed at the freedom you could find in each day, if every minute wasn't scheduled. If days were just days, instead of twenty-four-hour time-sensitive to-do lists.

I know. Everything on your calendar is super important. Absolutely! But is it more important than free time with your family?

Is it more important than sleep or self care? Is it so important you're willing to teach your children that? Most parents obviously want what is best for their children. So often I hear, "I want my kids to have more than I had, so I'm sacrificing now." But don't forget your children need you right now, probably more than they need "more than you had." Don't forget instead of teaching your children to enjoy that "more" later, you're likely just teaching them to make the same sacrifices you make.

I know. Your kids love soccer, or dance, or gymnastics, or wrestling. They also love pudding, but you don't let pudding control your life. Our kids loved soccer, baseball, basketball, and football, but we quickly realized those were consuming our entire life. A few games, practices, meetings, picture days, and parties, and suddenly the calendar said it was time for the next sport. Months had passed and, while we spent most every day going to and from the field or court, we spent very little time just being together. That was not going to work for our family. They were not likely headed to professional sports, so we decided not to spend twelve years on them. But they need to learn teamwork! Absolutely. And they can do that at a park, at church, at home, or even in one season of their favorite sport. Does teamwork really take twelve years to learn?

Am I saying sports are bad? Of course not. I loved them! I still do. Can they fit into a schedule without causing the whole family exhaustion and stress? Of course. But that might be difficult if you're also scheduling piano lessons, 4-H, scouts, and karate. Am I saying those extra curricular activities are bad then? Of course not. While each one of these opportunities are great individually, trying to do too many of them can be overwhelming for your children, you, and your entire family. As Stephen Covey says, "The key is not to prioritize what's on your schedule, but to schedule your priorities."[22]

Like unschooling, Allen wasn't quite as on board with unscheduling as me, especially when it came to sports. He was still hoping for the professional athlete child. He still is. It's not happening. Then again, Matt is an amazing climber at sixteen and he plans to continue advancing, so there's still hope for Allen. But like un-schooling, as we considered cutting out the sports, once again I assured him nothing was final. They could always start playing sports again. If they showed interest and talent, and especially if we saw professional potential, we could simply sign them up. The Cincinnati Reds would not say, "Oh, I'm sorry. We were going to sign your son, but we see here he didn't play baseball from age six to age twelve." And yes, the Reds or the Cincinnati Bengals would be our dream teams for our boys. That's how you know we're true fans. No, it's not easy loving Ohio teams, though the Ohio State Buckeyes do make up for it. Anyway, knowing we weren't com-pletely throwing away the chance for our kids to play for one of these beloved, or other lesser-loved professional teams, Allen again agreed. And our days became ours again.

What's funny is none of our kids miss soccer, baseball, basket-ball, or football at all. They got to play any of those in camp-grounds with their friends anytime they wanted. Since their friends were also nomadic and unscheduled, they had plenty of free time too. Once again, that trailblazer tribe formed and we would find our kids in heated games of tackle football in open fields. If some of the other kids felt like basketball or soccer, it would happen randomly. If some of the kids were serious about some sport, it would happen regularly. Even without the organ-ization, the kids still had plenty of the experiences.

So our kids had many opportunities for team sports, without the hectic schedules, although they did miss out on the snappy uniforms. Because they love adventure, and following Allen's lead, the kids really gravitated toward outdoor sports like white-water kayaking, climbing, rappelling, hiking, and canyoneering. It's interesting that, though these are more individual sports, they require much more teamwork than team sports. Maybe not more, maybe it's just to a different level. Team sports require teamwork to win games, while outdoor sports require teamwork to avoid death. That certainly doesn't take twelve years to learn.

Of course some of this depends on your goals. Do you want your kids to be physically fit and active? After our adventurous life, Josh breezed through thirteen weeks of Marine boot camp. Do you want your kids to have lots of trophies to display? Those are always fun. I loved looking at my father's trophies displayed on top of our piano as I grew up. I used to have that same goal, but my priorities shifted. I had many trophies from sports and 4-H and Allen had many from Taekwondo. While they were fun, we took pictures of them for the memories, and sold them in our auction when we hit the road. We haven't looked at the pictures since. Our kids kept a few trophies in the three trunks of mementos we kept, though they can't remember what they were and don't want them anymore. So do you want your kids to be active, have trophies, make friends, learn teamwork, collect uniforms, earn college scholarships, or play professional sports? If they're not likely heading to college and beyond, you may want to weigh the time spent versus the rewards. If they are, you may want to look at other areas where you can cut back.

What might your kids do if they had more free time? It's very likely they would do many of the things you stopped scheduling, without all the time, stress, and expense. Our kids learned guitar, ukulele, piano, and drums, without taking lessons. Musically inclined parents and friends are great resources, along with YouTube. They learned many of the ideals of 4-H by taking care of animals. They learned some of the community and outdoor principles of scouts, by living in community and spending time outdoors. They also learned a few karate moves, by fighting with each other, although I doubt that's a very good example. We're not perfect parents.

Your kids might also discover other interests if they had more free time. If they weren't busy each day, doing what they, or you, think they should be doing, they might get into robotics, theater, mechanics, or painting. They might find hobbies they enjoy far more than the ones no longer on the calendar. They might even find passions which change the course of their future. Of course they might just spend time climbing trees or playing games, which allow their brains much needed time to rest and recover.

One day we found Josh tanning a deer hide. I didn't even know that was a thing. Apparently you can learn how on YouTube. He also learned about military history from talking with veterans, four-wheeler mechanics from trial and error, and carpentry from building a barn with Allen. While it might sound like I'm back on the unschooling bandwagon (though isn't this a motivating argument?), this is about unscheduling. Your kids may find interests you would never think to add to your calendar. I've never seen a deer hide tanning class or a four-wheeler mechanics club personally. If Josh was busy with soccer, he might learn new plays, and he certainly would have the teamwork mastered, but he wouldn't have time for deer hides, military history, mechanics, or carpentry. And which will he use later in life anyway? As a hunter, a Marine, an old truck owner, and a future home owner, I think he'll be okay without the soccer plays.

Beyond the kids' sports, clubs, lessons, and activities, what about your own personal schedule? Do all of your opportunities actually feel like opportunities? Do they give you energy, fulfillment, and joy? Or do they feel more like obligations? Do they fill you with dread, resentment, and annoyance? Yes, they are probably all good opportunities. But are they all good-for-you opportunities? Are they actually good for you? Are they good for you right now, in this season of life? Were they better for you in the past? Would they be better for you in the future? Would they be better for someone else? Are they good for your family? Would your family agree?

I realize that was a ridiculous amount of questions in one paragraph. But I've also realized so many people have never stopped to think about any of these. So many are just adding each new "good opportunity" to a blank spot in the calendar, without evaluating what's already on there. Is that you? If so, I encourage you to go back, re-read the paragraph above, and honestly answer each of the questions. There's no rush, so take your time. Unless you're squeezing in some book reading time in between events on your busy calendar of course!

After really looking honestly at your busy schedule, does the thought of cutting back scare you? What if you took baby steps?

Maybe cancel one event or responsibility to free up a few hours one night each week. Would your family enjoy a peaceful dinner and a game or movie every Tuesday night? Take a hard look at your calendar and see if anything can go. Truthfully, everything could go. Our blank-calendared-life is proof of that, but I'm talking about baby steps here. I'm not saying everything should go either, so don't jump on that email just yet. (Wait until I make you mad in a few more chapters, then send it.) But is there one activity you've been doing, simply because it's on your calendar? Is there something you've lost the passion for, or that is no longer even needed, or that someone else may be praying for the opportunity to lead? Are you still going to the toddler mama group, but no longer have toddlers? Maybe you could just meet a friend for coffee. Are you on the landscaping committee, but notice Barb seems to make the best decisions and enjoy working alone? Maybe you could promote Barb to landscape artist and let yourself off the hook. Are you taking cookies to the nursing home, but quickly dropping them off because Wednesdays are so busy for you? Maybe Betsy, who's been lonely and praying for company, would love the chance to bake and then spend a few hours having conversations with new friends.

Is the idea of cutting back still scary or does it sound appealing? Would you like a little more breathing room in your day? If you're looking for freedom, you'll find it in letting go. Again, you don't have to completely clear your calendar, unless you want to. But you can bless others, bless your family, and bless yourself by doing a little less. With an open schedule, you will also be more available to help others when unexpected situations arise.

Because our calendar is wide open, we've had some great opportunities. We've been able to help friends during the daytime, when others weren't able to take off work. We've been available on weekends, because we weren't recovering from a busy week. We've also been able to completely change directions and rush to a funeral, attend a wedding, meet a new baby, help with tornado clean-up, flee smoke from wildfires, help remodel an RV, and so much more. When our calendar is not full of our activities, we can focus on blessing others. Instead of asking how we can best use today, we ask how we can best be used today.

Some of the opportunities have even been crazy. Recently we were in the right place, at the right time, with the total time freedom to help rescue a stolen puppy! Since it's still under investigation, the details will be a little vague, but our rescue mission was an adorable English Bulldog puppy! Through a strange series of events, we learned about a puppy stolen from Chicago in December and found in Los Angeles in February. Crazy, right?! But on the weekend the detectives found him, the owners couldn't get him from California back to Illinois for various reasons. Because I didn't see a reason why not, I said we could go get him. I mentioned I would run the idea by Allen, but I knew he'd be up for an adventure. We were currently in Las Vegas, it's only four hours away, and we had nothing else to do. The owners were shocked, but it sounded like fun to us. So the details were worked out between owners and detectives in Chicago and detectives in Los Angeles as we hopped in the truck and started driving. We drove to Los Angeles and met and fell in love with a very cute, very large little guy. Matt and the puppy bonded on the four hour drive home, napping together on the back seat. We brought him back to the RV in Las Vegas and got to keep him overnight. We'd forgotten how much work puppies were, so he's lucky he's cute! Our dog Jack was definitely not a fan, but they learned to coexist. We cuddled with the wrinkly ball of muscle, soaked up all the puppy cuteness, and then sent him off on the next leg of his trip home. He had two more stops, but is now home safe and sound in Illinois. We didn't try to keep him, no matter how much Matt begged. Those two did hit it off very well, but this guy had a long trip to finish. We were so glad we had the time and freedom so we could be a tiny part in this pup's incredible journey!

Some opportunities have been more purposeful and took longer to plan than a few hours. One year we took a big detour when we changed directions and headed to Joplin, Missouri to help clean up after the EF5-rated tornado. We were actually on the East coast and headed north to Maine. That was our plan anyway. We RVers like to say our plans are set in Jell-O because they change so often. We hadn't even heard of Joplin until the news of the devastating tornado on May 22, 2011. From the reports, photos, and videos, we knew there would be a great need for help, and thought it would be a good opportunity for our whole family. We also waited a month before going. We heard from so many that lots of volunteers show up to help immediately after disasters, but are only able to stay for a few weeks. Many said there would be so much help still needed and so few helpers after that, and they were certainly right.

We arrived in Joplin on a Monday and drove through the city. We'd been reading about the damage and looking at pictures and videos, but nothing prepares you for the reality of it. The tornado was a mile wide, and it went for miles, though neighborhoods, businesses, schools, and medical buildings. Seeing houses completely gone with even the basements exposed made us wonder how anyone survived at all. It was mile after mile of just unbelievable devastation. We looked forward to helping, but it was overwhelming.

While we brought ten helping hands with our family of five, it turned out having a whole family would make it a little more difficult. Most organizations didn't allow children under eighteen to help at all, so it took some digging. Another difficulty was finding the information before we got there. Many places didn't answer calls or emails, so we weren't sure of our plans, or even if we would be able to help at all, until we arrived. Once we did, we visited many sites and asked around until we found enough information to give us some options.

Fortunately, there were plenty of opportunities to keep us busy and let us be useful with our many helpful (but young) hands. AmeriCorps, based at Missouri Southern State University, had some collection centers which allowed children, as long as they were supervised. It was a warehouse environment with forklifts, trucks, equipment, etc. There were a lot of donations coming in by the truckload and all of them had to be sorted, repacked, and labeled to send out to be distributed. Forest Park

Baptist Church had some moving, sorting, and packing work at their makeshift warehouse/bus garage. Joplin Family Worship Center had a collection and distribution center that needed lots of help, and our children were welcome. We did a lot of sorting and stocking of a makeshift pantry, where Joplin residents could come to get basic supplies, cleaning products, toiletries, clothes, food, and water. The Salvation Army had a similar pantry and welcomed our whole family. Lizzy and I sorted and stocked clothes and shoes. Allen's forklift experience came in handy and he rocked the forklift all day. Josh helped him work outside, sorting pallets. Matt helped us, Allen, his new favorite friend Mr. Mel, some very pretty volunteer girls, some residents needing assistance, and pretty much anyone who needed it, or didn't need it. He was also quite helpful getting inside the huge boxes to hand things out.

One day, after a full day's work, we went to pass out dinners from the Joplin Family Worship Center. The kids had been hoping for the chance to hand out food in the city and were excited and full of energy somehow. Joplin Family provided roast beef, mashed potatoes, gravy, corn, bread, cookies, and water and sent us to find hungry people. We found very grateful people working and living in the disaster area. It was incredibly sobering seeing the houses close-up and knocking on their doors (if they still had doors).

At first, we were disappointed that we couldn't take the kids out into the field to work. Allen spent time helping out there without us, though, and we better understood why they couldn't. We saw the damage first hand as we passed out meals. Then Allen told us all about his experience, working to removing debris with each step littered with dangerous nails and sharp metal and wood pieces everywhere. So we ended up being very grateful they couldn't!

We enjoyed being able to help, though it was often bittersweet. We heard heartbreaking stories, worked alongside victims who had lost everything, and saw firsthand how the tornado affected the residents of Joplin. There was also a lot of fun and laughter as volunteers and victims alike tried to make the best of a sad situation with humor. We highly recommend helping out as you can at locations near you, or as you travel. It's certainly a worthy cause, appreciated by the locals, and quite an experience for adults and children of all ages.

One of our favorite parts of our time helping there in Missouri was working alongside two other traveling families. We had met the Godwin and Igel families separately, earlier in the year, and both had decided to help in Joplin. So we joined them, and among our three families alone, we brought eighteen helpers! Since they also had location and time freedom, we got to spend a few weeks working, laughing, learning, and helping collectively. It's always fun when trailblazers come together.

Thanks to that trailblazer tribe, we've been able to spend so much quality and quantity time with other families and friends who live mostly unscheduled too. We didn't even know they existed as we first started cutting activities from our schedule. We thought our family was the only one bold enough, or crazy enough, to slow down and turn in our "I'm so busy" badges. But they were easy to spot because they were at the playgrounds, parks, movies, and stores during the middle of the day or in the afternoon when most families were running ragged. It was comforting to learn we weren't alone. They helped us feel we were on the best path for our family and we wouldn't be traveling it alone. And indeed we haven't. We've shared so many fun times with other families who also left their calendars open.

Before we hit the road, we found a few other homeschooling families and took field trips to nature centers, environmental education centers, waterfalls, hikes, parks, and musicals. On the road, there are so many more people with time freedom. The younger families are almost all homeschooling and working remotely and the older ones are mostly retired. So potlucks, pool times, games, campfires, and conversations can happen any time of the day in campgrounds. And field trips to national parks, historical sites, amusement parks, rivers, and beaches can happen any time of the day outside campgrounds. While I'm writing

today, Allen and another dad, who we just met in this campground, are taking all the kids for a hike in beautiful Red Rock Canyon outside of Las Vegas, Nevada. Because no one is busy, they can
go on a random Thursday before it gets crowded on the weekend.
We've had so much fun with other nomadic families at places
like Walt Disney World, Universal Studios, NASA, Gateway Arch
in St. Louis, the Grand Canyon, Mount Rushmore, Zion National
Park, Acadia National Park, and dozens of other national parks
and monuments. But we've also had great times in silly, helpful,
or deep conversations right in the campgrounds. We're so grateful
for all the friends we've made who also see the value in unscheduling.

Since it's not common to not be busy, many people don't
even understand the concept. I had a funny conversation with a
woman who called to schedule an appointment with me over the
phone. I tried to be helpful and let her set the day and time, since
it didn't matter to me. But that didn't seem to help.

Caller: "When is a good time for you?"
Me: "Any time on any day is fine here."
Caller: "Which day is best?"
Me: "Any day."
Caller: "Would Thursday work?"
Me: "Yes."
Caller: "Would a different day be better?"
Me: "Literally any day is fine."
Caller: "Okay, so Thursday then?"
Me: "Yes."
Caller: "So what time is best?"
Me: "Literally any time is fine."
Caller: "Would 2pm work?"
Me: "Yes."
Caller: "Would a different time be better?"
Me: "No, that is perfect. Thursday at 2pm. It's on my calendar."
Caller: "Just let me know if you need to change it."
Me: "No, that is the only time I'm available that whole week. It's
absolutely perfect."

Caller: "Well, I'm glad it worked out."

Me: "Me too." But I was thinking "Oh my dear goodness, please let this conversation end."

I knew she was trying to be considerate of our schedule and appreciated it, but I don't think she ever understood we didn't have one.

While not everyone understands it, and it may not be common in your world, unscheduling really is freeing. Whether you're looking for time to breathe or time to be more available for opportunities, trimming your schedule will help. Completely clearing your schedule will bring more freedom than you would know what to do with, which is a lovely way to live in my opinion. But even if you're not ready for that, I'm guessing you would like a little less exhaustion and stress in your day. You can find that by letting go. Just let go of a little and see how it feels. Enjoy that taste of freedom! You can hang on tightly to your "I'm so busy" badge, or you could set it aside for safe keeping, just for a little while. Remember, nothing is final. You can always grab that badge, pull out your colored pens, and fill up your calendar again. But maybe you're ready to let go. Maybe you want to try being a trailblazer with your schedule. If so, there will be a tribe there to help.

CHAPTER 6: UNDIETING

Allen and I married in 1997 and quite honestly, we steadily gained weight ever since. Isn't that what married people do? Sadly, if you look around, that really is the example you see. That seemed normal and since we were keeping up with the Joneses, we followed right along. We were still active. We loved playing sports like softball and volleyball. We joined leagues and worked out. We also gained ten pounds, and then twenty.

So we did what the Joneses were doing. We complained, a lot. We lamented the loss of our teenage metabolism. We couldn't believe with all our physical activity, our bodies would betray us by continuing to pack on the pounds. We dieted. We exercised. We bought the equipment and really tried to use it. It got dusty. We joined a gym and went for a while. It got old. We did a cabbage soup diet where we could eat as much as we wanted, but it was just soup. It didn't even taste good. It was as bad as it sounds. We bought diet pills and were shocked they didn't decrease our appetite. We couldn't believe a television ad would not be truthful and used the money-back guarantee. We tried counting calories, eating raw, and so much more, but year after year, we were still fat. And getting fatter.

Don't get me wrong. We were fat and happy, mostly. We weren't completely miserable. We still played ball, hiked, kayaked, and kept up with the kids. When we hit the road in 2010, our health didn't keep us from enjoying our adventures. We took all-day paddling trips down rivers and always hiked to the tops of mountains. The kids did make fun of my constant need to "stop and take pictures" though. We all knew that was just my excuse to get my heart rate and breathing under control. Despite my slow pace and "picture" delays though, I always made it to the top, eventually. Allen needed a larger kayak to accommodate his belly, but he never missed a chance to run a river. He kayaked class V rapids like a pro too, so his weight obviously didn't keep him from his crazy adventures.

So we were fat and happy, until we weren't. In 2014 and 2015 we really slowed down. We had never had a home base before, but for those two years we really sat still for the majority of the time. You will read about our Arkansas unhomesteading adventures in a later chapter. Our time unhomesteading was wonderful, but we didn't do very much because we simply didn't feel like it. We thought we had lost our sense of adventure. We had done so much all across the country and figured maybe we had just seen it all. Maybe we were just finished. We settled into being boring and content. Of course we did go south for the winter, because we still didn't like snow. When you get used to chasing 70°F year-round, it's hard to ever put up with snow again!

So we went to Texas, where we met our friends, the Johnsons, who I mentioned in the unworking and unlocating chapters. We've had a lot of fun together! We had watched them rapidly shrinking in their photos on social media, so we knew they were getting healthy. But I assumed they were doing a fad diet or using some magic pills, which I had no interest in. I even told Allen not to ask what they did for a living, though it's a common question, because they would try to sell us something. Since Allen is much more polite than me, he asked anyway. I kicked him under the table and they saw me. I'm not polite or apparently subtle either. They've come to love me anyway, though! How could they not? Add humble to that list, I guess. Answering his question, they said they were transformation coaches and shared how much they loved it. And much to my surprise, they didn't try to sell us anything.

So we just had fun together in the campground, mostly playing pickleball. Google that sport if you haven't heard of it yet. It's really fun! Since we were starting to be more active again, and feeling the effects of that, we finally felt like we really needed to make some changes. We wanted to get healthy, but our past experiences proved we certainly didn't know how. So we decided to see how the Johnsons did it.

They shared how they simply dialed in their nutrition to lose weight, and we were amazed! They weren't on a fad diet. There were no pills, wraps, or supplements. They just ate food, six times a day, and drank a lot of water. That sounded like the opposite of dieting to me, more like undieting. And not dieting sounded very appealing. We already knew dieting didn't work for very long. They said what really mattered was what we ate and when we ate it. It made a lot of sense, but I was still skeptical.

I explained that we knew what healthy eating was. I shared how we ate completely natural food in Arkansas. They were far too kind to point out that we were still fat! I might have deserved that, but they knew it was my journey. But I did realize that myself as I considered it. I still crack up thinking about my mindset back then. Yes, our meat was all natural and our veggies were straight from the garden, but we weren't losing weight. We were maintaining our fat. So Allen and I discussed it more seriously. It honestly sounded too easy, but we decided to give it one month. What did we have to lose?

Well, in one month, Allen and I lost quite a bit of weight, and indeed it was too easy! We felt great right away. It had been decades, so we'd forgotten how good it feels to be healthy. We had fewer aches and pains. We had more energy, patience, and clarity. And best of all, we had our sense of adventure back! We felt free again! We no longer wanted to sit still, so we hit the road and headed west. We enjoyed hiking again and exploring interesting places with the kids. We were excited to share new adventures and we actually had the stamina needed for them. The adventurous spirit of freedom we once had was back, stronger than ever.

We both hit our goals in only five months and actually weighed less than we did when we were married! A few months earlier, we didn't realize that was even possible. We got back down to our high school weights, believe it or not, because it's actually still hard for us to believe! Three years later, we are still at those same weights, thanks to our new healthy habits and to the accountability of helping others reach their goals.

Our new habits have made all the difference. That is why the nutrition program we used beat any diet we tried. A diet usually means going without something. And they are not often sustainable. So once they're over, most people will go back to their former habits. With our program, we started changing our habits from the first day. And our coaches were there to help us undo our thinking about dieting. They became part of the trailblazer tribe.

We changed how, when, what, and why we ate. We learned about how and when to fuel our bodies. We ate more often, while learning what to eat. And we learned why all of it mattered. But I think the best part was that, while we were learning all of this, our program was very easy. We knew exactly what to do, while soaking up all the new knowledge. We also saw results immediately, so we were encouraged to keep going. It's easy to stick to a plan that is simple, yummy, and effective. We felt great, were never hungry, had no cravings, and slept better. At that point, we knew our goals were actually possible. That was freedom!

We looked at water differently too. We were encouraged to drink at least sixty-four ounces a day, but to aim higher. A common rule of thumb is to drink at least half your body weight in ounces. So Allen and I were both drinking one hundred ounces a day. We still are, out of habit. But we changed our thinking. I used to think, though not very frequently, "I'm thirsty. I need water." Now I think about all the benefits of water, like boosting metabolism, cleansing of waste, suppressing appetite, decreasing water retention, and helping metabolize fat. Now I just think, "I want those benefits. I want water." So drinking water throughout the day is just another healthy habit we've continued.

Once we reached our weight loss goals, we went through a transition from losing weight to maintaining our weight. This was the key for us, because we didn't want to go back to our former habits and gain it back! We still ate six times a day, but we added more nutrition for our goals. We each learned what we needed for our specific height, weight, and lifestyle. And of course our coaches helped.

We still eat that way, three years later. We're not on a diet. We just eat food. We don't eat perfectly every day and we certainly aren't willing to go without our favorites on occasion. We just have really good days before and after those splurges. It's funny, because I used to worry about not ever having the unhealthy things I loved. But now, most of those things don't even taste good to me anymore. Our bodies have really adjusted to being fueled well and they crave healthy things!

Our relationship with food is very different now. We learned about emotional, habitual, and bored eating and how to make healthier choices for our benefit. Instead of mindless eating, we mindfully consider our options. We ask if that option would be helpful to us or not. If not, we ask if that option would be worth it or not. Sometimes we think it is and we indulge. For example, hot dogs and apple pie on the opening day of baseball season was absolutely worth it to us. That's simply being a good American, especially if you cheer for the Cincinnati Reds. But a leftover donut on a random Tuesday would not be worth it to us. The only kind of donut worth it would be a fresh, hot off the belt, glazed donut that melts in your mouth. Although it would only be worth it if we had some really good days before. We try to have healthy days the majority of the time, in case that donut option ever appears. We obviously have a donut problem in the Lundy family. But now we recognize this and avoid donut shops, for the most part. Because a life without donuts would be meaningless, though, we indulge in the occasional sweet goodness. But we buy one donut each now, instead of one dozen. Since health is our habit now, we stop there and don't let it get out of control. And it feels really good to be in control again, after all these years.

The accountability of helping others has also kept us on track. The thought of gaining five or ten pounds myself doesn't bother me too much honestly. But the thought of who is watching me does! I know there are people working toward getting healthy because of major health scares. And others are making changes to inspire their entire families. To me, it would mean my clothes feeling a little tight. To others, it might mean dying young. That is some powerful motivation to know my consistency and example can help others live longer. They often don't believe in themselves yet, so I get to show them it's possible. Allen and I like feeling great, but more importantly, we love seeing others feeling great.

Because we changed our habits and are dedicated to being great examples for others, we've been able to help thousands of people on their health journeys. We've watched people lose a few pounds to a few hundred pounds. We've seen them reduce or eliminate medications. We've cheered as they've grown in confidence and ability, taking part in their favorite activities again. We've cried as we've listened to stories of people so grateful for getting their lives back. Well, I have. Allen doesn't really cry, but they hit him right in the feels.

Even though we're very motivated to stay on track, we're certainly not perfect. We've allowed a few holidays or family visits here and there to veer us off course a little. Fortunately, we know how to use nutrition to quickly get back on track. We can stay focused on our nutrition for a week or two and be right back at our goal weights. It's an awesome feeling to have that kind of information and power. That is freedom!

I once went on a mom's cruise and decided to make mostly good choices. I didn't have Allen to keep me accountable, but I wanted to feel good and not pay for it on the scales. If you haven't been on one, a cruise ship is really just a fancy, floating buffet. There are endless buffets, grills, specialty restaurants, and room service, plus pizza and ice cream cones available twenty-four hours a day. And all of this is free! That is a lot of temptation for a food addict, but I knew my new habits would help. I wasn't perfect, but I was mindful about my meals. I started with a lot of healthy things like protein and vegetables, so I wouldn't be very hungry. Then I took very small portions of the unhealthy things, so I could just have a taste of each. I went very light on desserts too, sampling only the best ones. That way I enjoyed myself, without overdoing it. I also took the stairs every time and drank a lot of water, so I got plenty of exercise and hydration. After that five-day cruise, I gained four pounds. That wasn't perfect, but it wasn't bad. With just four days of careful nutrition back at home, those four pounds were gone!

On our next cruise, Allen came with me. We decided to see what would happen if we just went crazy. Because we were usually careful, we really weren't sure how much weight we might gain. Remember the free, floating buffet? That made this experiment potentially dangerous. But we went and enjoyed ourselves thoroughly. We indulged and ate ourselves silly. We stuffed our faces until we couldn't anymore. Then we went back for ice cream cones. We acted like the food addicts we are. It wasn't pretty. And we felt like crap. While it was fun for the first few days, we already regretted our choices. Our bodies were letting us know they were unhappy. Read between those lines if you dare. The results of our experiment were interesting. More important than any weight we gained, we simply didn't think it was worth it to feel so bad. It was a good reminder of how bad we used to feel, and a good lesson on how badly we never want to feel that way again. We did pay for it on the scales too. We each gained eight pounds! It was only a four day cruise. Like I said, it wasn't pretty. Fortunately, after two weeks of focus and refreshingly wonderful food, those sixteen pounds were history. It felt so good to feel good again!

If we go on another cruise, which is highly likely, I think we'll do great. It was good to gather that data and learn what could happen. I'm actually glad we did it, now that it's over. It's great motivation now to just be thankful for the wide variety of healthy foods available and focus on enjoying all the shows, activities, and other amenities on the ship. Our many previous cruises were all before we got healthy, so those were not very pretty either. Back then, though, we ate like that every day. And back then, we didn't understand nutrition, so those extra pounds just stayed with us each time. I have a feeling there will be more cruising in our future. They're just such great options, with one low price that covers everything, including lodging, travel, entertainment, sight-seeing, and of course food. Though next time, we'll enjoy the healthy food!

We have always, quite obviously, enjoyed our food. One of our concerns, when we decided to get healthy, was meals would be boring and no longer fun. Allen likes to say eating used to be a full contact sport. He's not exaggerating. If it was no longer a sport around here, would it still be fun? We loved trying new things in new areas as we traveled too. We didn't want to give that up. We didn't want to be high-maintenance customers every time we ate at restaurants either. We thought we would have a very short list of acceptable meals. We also thought they would be bland and uninteresting. I'm not sure why we were so concerned. Plenty of healthy people appear to have fun lives. So we were very pleasantly surprised to learn healthy eating could indeed be fun. It's very fun actually!

We still love food. Who doesn't? But now we love it, without the guilt! We've discovered so many new foods and ways to prepare old favorites. We're now big fans of spaghetti squash and cauliflower. Who knew you could grow noodles in your garden? Well, you probably did, but we didn't! And we thought cauliflower was just for dipping in ranch dressing, when the broccoli ran out. We had no idea it could turn into pizza crust, bread sticks, bagels, rice, mashed potatoes, tater tots, potato soup, macaroni and cheese, or tortillas. That is a magical vegetable. For more magic tricks, we also learned to turn eggs and cream cheese into bread, turn almonds into milk, and bread chicken without using bread.

Still being able to enjoy our favorite foods was important to us too. Of course those favorites have changed considerably as our bodies adjusted to the good stuff. But we still have pizza at least once a week. Now the crust is just made with meat, zucchini, spaghetti squash, or cauliflower. Meat crust pizza is our favorite because it's yummy, easy, and requires very little preparation. We also have chicken stir-fry often, with broccoli, onions, peppers, and cauliflower rice. The first time I made that, I didn't tell the kids it was cauliflower and they didn't even notice! Lasagna is still a favorite, but with spaghetti squash or zucchini instead of pasta. We eat a variety of salads, and especially love taco salad.

We even fry and then bake faux-breaded chicken that tastes like Kentucky Fried Chicken. Healthy KFC is just crazy! We've enjoyed these healthy meals so much over the years. Our teenagers have as well, so you know they're good. Many of our favorite recipes are on our website if you're interested.

Restaurant etiquette was another concern. Fortunately, for our first healthy meal away from home, we were camping with the Johnsons, so we knew they would help. We went to the Fort Worth Stockyards and had a great day together. When we got to the restaurant, we were nervous and glad they were there. We didn't know what to order and what special requests we might have to make. So we let them do it all and sat back to learn. But they just ordered a chicken salad without croutons and dressing on the side. That was ridiculously easy. And it's been easy ever since. We even received a guide to help, though we don't even need it anymore. We like ordering things at restaurants we're not likely to have at home. Since Allen's a bass fisherman, we never have salmon, so that's my first choice. Since I don't like steak, and we no longer have unlimited deer steaks, I rarely make that at home, so that's Allen's first choice.

Trying new things as we travel, using our "when in Rome" attitude, has been easy too. We sometimes choose to make healthy choices at highly recommended restaurants. Or if the area's famous specialty isn't healthy, then we use the question method, asking if it would be helpful, then if it would be worth it. So, we definitely enjoy food still, whether we make it at home or go out to eat. We are so glad healthy meals are not boring as we had feared. So we love healthy food, we can still enjoy unhealthy food occasionally, and we can course correct as needed. And we can do this while remaining at our goal weight and feeling great. That is total health freedom!

It didn't take very long to begin learning about healthy eating either, because we had a trailblazer tribe to help. We found great encouragement, along with yummy recipes. It's so nice when people share their successes and failures in the kitchen before you try it out. Because we weren't dieting, and we were undoing everything we thought about dieting, it was great to have help. We were changing our lifestyle, not just our portion sizes. That could be overwhelming, so we're very thankful the tribe made it easy and fun.

We noticed some differences as soon as we started eating better, besides just feeling and looking better. We were no longer worn out after a meal. Do you ever feel like you need a nap after dinner? We always did. And I always thought that was normal. I thought your body just needed time to process all that food and it was a big job. Well, with all the food we used to eat, it was a very big job! After healthy meals now, we feel satisfied, but not stuffed. We feel refreshed and ready to keep moving. It feels like we've properly fueled our bodies up, instead of bogging them down.

We had a lot more energy throughout the day as well. I was used to the ups and downs and thought that's how bodies functioned. I'd have bursts of energy after caffeine, then drag until lunch. That would get me by for a while, then I'd feel like I needed an afternoon nap. I now understand my energy would cycle up and down with my blood sugar. Now that we eat better food and more frequently, our sugar levels stay consistent and we don't have the spikes and dips. So we feel good and have plenty of energy all day. That is very convenient if you want to put in a hard day of work or play.

We also experienced some unexpected things, like mental clarity and patience. I definitely felt that brain fog lift, and I've heard the same from so many others. My focus and concentration improved greatly and I could think clearly. Brain fog is often attributed to stress, sleep, hormones, or medical conditions. Many say it's because they have kids. I'll admit I've said that. Of course nutrition helps with most of those things anyway, except for kids. But patience can help with kids and that improved as well. It was fascinating that as I felt better, I acted better. It makes sense to me now, looking back and having seen it happen to so many people. Back then though, I was just amazed at how amazing I could be. It made me realize our kids deserve me to be the best me I can be!

Just by watching and listening to us, now our kids have some great tools for the future. We have given them a great education and they understand nutrition better than most adults. I wish I would have had that kind of knowledge at that age. While Allen and I didn't really know how to start, our kids will know exactly what to do if they decide they need to focus on their health. Lizzy even used our program to lose fifteen pounds a few years ago and is holding steady. Of course we hope they will just continue to use these healthy habits, but they are teenagers. Even if they don't though, they will know how to get back on track. Maybe we'll even be lucky enough to hear the words, "You were right." We do love hearing that.

So after all our dieting and traditional attempts to lose weight failed, we finally learned undieting was the answer. We now understand nutrition and know what to eat and when to eat it. We didn't have to diet at all! We simply changed our lifestyle and learned how to eat. And as usual, we learned it all with help from our tribe of trailblazers.

I can't tell you right now exactly what you should do to get healthy, because I don't know your current reality or your future goals. If you want to chat over tea, or email, I'd be happy to point you in the right direction. Just contact me, because I'd love to meet you. Unless you're a weirdo. Though some of my favorite people are weirdos, so maybe I should say especially if you're a weirdo. I can tell you, though, undieting will probably change your life. If you undo everything you think about dieting, like we did, and start developing healthy habits, your future could be full of health freedom too.

CHAPTER 7: UNFRIENDING

When we hit the road, we were a little worried about losing friends. So were our kids. So are many people who are currently considering a nomadic lifestyle, according to the frequent questions we receive and read online. In our little farmhouse in Troy, we had a great community, a church family, fellow homeschooling families, and friends we could count on. We knew we would not actually be unfriending our friends, but we also knew it wouldn't be the same. We'd moved before and we knew the drill. We wouldn't gather together regularly. We would have less in common. We would drift apart. It happens. It's happened to us enough times that we knew what to expect. What we didn't know this time, though, was what to expect after that. After each move to a new town, we eventually made friends, found a church family, and formed a community. We had no idea what would happen if we didn't move to a new town. If there was no new destination, would we just be alone as we explored the country? Would we make friends quickly and then sadly leave a week later? Would we resist even making friends to avoid the heartbreak of leaving them? Would we cling more tightly to our current friends online? Would our kids ever have playmates? What about best friends as they got older? We simply had no idea. We knew a life of adventure was calling us, but this unfriending part was an unknown. We also knew freedom was found in the unknown and help would come. So we took the step and were amazed.

During our first month, we camped with friends. During our second, we visited old friends and made new ones. Our third brought more old friends and more new ones. The longer we went, and the farther we went, the more we reconnected with old friends and connected with new ones. The kids would see an RV with a bunkhouse or bicycles and go make friends. They were ten,

ten, and seven then, so that wasn't awkward yet. They would find friends on the playgrounds or in the pools, and we would meet the parents. We were rarely known as Margie or Allen. We were Josh's mom or Lizzy's dad. Most frequently we were asked if we were that little blond boy's parents. We always asked why first, because it was Matt. That usually went in one of two directions. It either started with he's so cute or we have a little problem. But that's understandable, because he was seven. And because he was Matt. We're still asked that question today and we still ask why first. Because he's still Matt.

Once, a lady drove to our campsite in a golf cart. She asked if the little blond boy lived there. We asked why and braced for the answer. It's a habit. She said she promised to bake him cupcakes and wanted to deliver them while they were still hot. Things like that happened often, because he can be a charmer. Another lady, not quite as friendly, came to report the little blond boy was jumping off the swings. Things like that happened often too, because he's a kid. It probably didn't help that we had contests for swing jumping. Oops. One time we passed a man in a campground and he and Matt greeted each other like old friends. I asked who he was and Matt said, "Oh, he's the guy from the dumpster." The guy from the dumpster?! It turns out he had been helping Matt each time he took the trash to the dumpster. They were camped close to it and saw Matt struggling to get the bag up and over, so he helped. Then he started watching for Matt coming, and helped him every day. Since then, we got to know them and even visited with them in other states. So Matt was an asset, and sometimes a liability, in helping us make friends.

We were definitely an oddity in the campground, since we had kids there in the middle of the week, when most were in school. So we hit it off well with the other oddities we met along the way. As usual, we started finding the trailblazers. We met one RVing family on the top of Mount Rushmore, when both of us literally parked under the presidents' noses. We spent a fun week together, just hanging out and getting to know each other. Another family put on a concert in our campground during our first winter in

Florida and our kids are still friends today. We ran into one family as we were both parked in a Walmart parking lot. We camped with them in four different states, once in the driveway of their house. Sometimes we spent a few days with friends, sometimes a few months. Some families we've met once and lost touch with over the years. Some we've stayed in contact with and chat often. Some we've run into all over the country, camping together in multiple states. While we worried our freedom would prevent friendships, we've found even more than we imagined.

A few families we've known since shortly after we hit the road in 2010, so we've watched each others' kids grow up. Some are back in houses and others are still on the road. We've seen some of the kids get married, have babies, get jobs, join the military, or go to college. While it's not a physical community, it sure feels like one. We didn't know how much this trailblazer tribe would come to mean to us.

We had no idea a nomadic community could even exist. Isn't that an oxymoron? According to Google, nomads are "people having no permanent abode"[23] and community means "a group of people living in the same place."[24] Yet somehow our community of nomads is stronger than any community we've experienced living in non-moving houses in non-moving towns. It's also a very large community of thousands of other traveling families! They've become our tribe.

Nomadic life is often hard to explain to house livers. For almost four decades, I was a house liver, and I never would have understood. I would have thought it was crazy. Sometimes I still think it is, although I love it. As a former house liver, I will attempt to explain some of the social differences between those who live in houses and those who live on the road, and how they affect friendship.

Once you hit the road, you shed a lot of the social rules you were used to living by. When you find another traveling family, you connect so much faster because you're both weird. (Not weird-weird, though we have met many weird people on the road, and many weird people who live in houses.) But weird as in you've both already left the social norms to even be there. You've both already decided you're willing to live with your children in a small box 24/7/365. You've both already decided you're okay with being weird.

So it's nothing like walking up to a stranger at the grocery store and asking them to hang out that night at your house. That would be so awkward. It's very different. You can make some assumptions. You should never make assumptions, though, right? I don't want to assume you make assumptions. But let's assume you do. You can assume family time is very important to your new friends. You can assume they embrace home education. You can assume they work from home or have saved money for travel. You can assume they had to leave friends and family too. You can assume they don't have a local church community. You can assume they have an open schedule and will have time to spend around a campfire. Most importantly, you can assume they will not judge you for your lifestyle. They won't even ask you to explain your lifestyle. They will understand it completely.

They won't ask you how you can stand being with your kids all day. They won't quiz your children on the multiplication table or ask you, "What about socialization?" They won't ask if you hit the lottery or if you need some cash because you must be destitute. They won't ask how you could leave friends and church families because they will understand. They won't even ask the common RVing questions, like "Do you have running water?" or "How do you cook meals?" or "Do you have a bed?" And yes, they will gladly visit around a campfire, getting to know you, and probably swapping stories about people asking the questions above. We don't even mind those questions. We understand. We used to ask them ourselves. It's very refreshing, though, not having to spend time explaining our philosophy of life before we exchange names.

Since all of that is out of the way, you can have deeper conversations about the meaning of life or the meaning of tow ratings. You can discuss common interests like favorite places to travel or favorite RV accessories. Even politics and religion aren't as taboo in the nomadic world, because with a mutual lack of judgment, conversations can be open and productive.

When you meet fellow travelers, all of those assumptions quickly pass through your mind, and you greet them with a smile. When you say, "Hello!" it really means, "Hello! I'm so glad to know you get me and I get you and now we can fast forward to see if we'll be great friends!" Sometimes you will, and sometimes you won't, as with any friendship. The process is just so much faster than when we moved to new towns. It took so much time and effort to identify people who might be potential friends, and even longer getting to know them to see if they were indeed potential friends. Nomads can skip all of that and just say, "Hello!" Maybe we will hit if off and spend hours around a campfire. Or maybe we won't and we'll say, "See you later!" with a smile, at least appreciating that there's another family out there who gets us.

Finding those other families makes nomadic life so much better for the kids and adults too. Of course social media makes it possible for us to meet and stay in contact with them. Fulltime-Families.com has made it even easier for the trailblazers to find each other too. Chris and Kimberly Travaglino started Fulltime Families when they hit the road, shortly after us in 2010. It's been a wonderful resource for RVers and a great way to find other families. Allen and I have made many friends, and we make a point to cross paths whenever possible. Lizzy, Josh, and Matt have made great friends on the road too. They get to meet up across the country as well. Seeing those friends gives us all that community feeling, no matter where we are.

The kids especially love winters in Florida, because most families migrate south. They get to spend months with the same friends every year, plus meet new ones. And Allen and I enjoy visiting with our friends, old and new, over tea or around campfires. Most of the families use the same membership campgrounds, so anytime between November and March, there may be fifty or more families in the same campground. That means a lot of friends! For the little kids, there are games, crafts, swimming, and movie nights. But mainly they just play all day every day. For the teenagers, they get to hang out, play video games, or long board. A favorite with ours is walking to a nearby gas station to buy junk food and hang out more. The adults take morning walks, help each other with maintenance, or share potluck meals. It definitely feels like a neighborhood, just with ever-changing neighbors as families move in and out of the campground.

Fulltime Families rallies and meet-ups are more opportunities to find many of our friends in one place. As I mentioned in the unlocating chapter, one rally had over eighty families, which added up to over three hundred people! Rallies are even more like neighborhoods, because everyone is parked together all week. So it's a very focused time of community and friendship. And it's really fun to watch this tribe in action. There are organized events, fun side trips, lots of free time to play, and spontaneous projects which pop up all over. We share meals, swap tools, take classes, and play games. At the kids' marketplace, the adults get to support the kids. And the kids get the chance to learn about business and marketing as they sell crafts, food, or other items. It's inspiring to see their creativity, but not too surprising, since they're all being raised by nomads.

One of my favorite parts of a rally is the parade of homes. We get to tour many of the RVs and see how other families organize and decorate. It's so fascinating to see the differences and fun to get new ideas for our own home. Allen loved bubble soccer, where the adults ran around in giant bubbles attempting to kick a ball. It was hilarious! Lizzy loves the dances, especially the 1980's themed prom. Everyone went all out, with crazy colors and big hair, and we had a blast. But they're always fun. Even the boys love dancing until the very end. Josh liked being around so many other people who did the same thing we did. It's not often we feel normal, but at rallies, we are indeed just like everyone else for a change. And Matt's favorite part is just all of the hanging out with friends. He doesn't care if they're doing something fun or doing nothing at all. He just enjoys the time with his friends. Undoing what we thought about having friends has really shown us a different kind of friendship. And we're all grateful for our friends on the road.

A cool part of nomadic life is that our friends aren't only people just like us. Sometimes they're families with similar situations and views. Sometimes they are families who are very different from us. Sometimes they aren't families at all. They may be younger or older, working or retired, or full-time RVers or weekend campers. They may have different opinions on politics, religion, vaccinations, climate change, or gun control, but most of our debates focus more on the best type of camper, tow vehicle, homeschooling, car seats, or chocolate to use in s'mores. We're not usually from the same town, state, or even country, so our backgrounds are vastly different too. When we lived in a house, most of our friends also grew up in Ohio and were close to our ages, because most of our kids were the same ages. It's been refreshing to have such a wide range in our nomadic community.

Some of the friends we love the most, probably also differ from us the most. We think some of their views are crazy! Of course they would say the same about us. But they're also the most kind, considerate, thoughtful, charitable, and fun people we know! Traveling has definitely led us to a bigger, broader, and I would even say better neighborhood, because we've been so blessed by a wide variety of friends.

We've been especially glad for our kids to grow up in this atmosphere. Instead of a classroom full of kids with the same ages and backgrounds, their world is so much bigger. Josh really enjoyed meeting veterans and they would talk for hours. Some were newly retired and in their forties, but most were over sixty. I'll never forget the time in an Arizona campground when an older gentleman knocked on the door and asked if Josh could come outside. It makes me tear up now. They had apparently talked about gunsmithing and he had some magazines to show Josh. They sat outside on the picnic table and it was so sweet. Josh also spent a lot of time playing his guitar with other musicians. He went to weekly bluegrass jams and played around many campfires. It was heartening to watch him with his friends of all ages.

Lizzy preferred to spend time with girls her own age, but she seemed to captivate the younger ones. They loved her and would follow her everywhere. Some mornings we would wake up to find one sitting on our front step of the RV, hoping Lizzy would come out to play soon. They didn't understand about teenagers sleeping until noon of course. She was so patient and accommodating. It was adorable. She actually gave away all of her toys to girls on the road. As she outgrew them, she gradually gave more away to the little girls she met.

As I mentioned, Matt made friends with many of the grandparent-types. He had grandfathers get out remote control cars to play with him and grandmothers give him rides on their golf carts. They even gave him paying jobs. Of course Matt also seemed inclined to befriend older girls too. Allen and I would often meet some teenage girls in campgrounds and they would already know Matt. Once at a waterpark, Matt said he'd met some friends in line and asked if he could go do the lazy river with them. We agreed and he took off. Then I realized our mistake. We should have asked him more about his friends. We ran into him again after a few hours, just Matt and a squad of bikini-clad high school cheerleaders on a field trip. He obviously keeps us on our toes.

While we love making new friends, it's also been fun to visit family and friends as we travel. Since my parents are in Florida, we get to see them almost every winter. Sometimes we winter out west, but we usually make it back to Florida by Thanksgiving or Christmas. Then we stay until March or April. It's been so nice for the kids to grow up getting to spend more time with their grandparents than just a vacation or two each year. I'm also quite glad they're so flexible with our lack of planning. My dad especially likes to joke about making plans, just so we can break them. This year they expected us to arrive in Florida possibly by January, or maybe March or April, unless we changed our minds. As usual, we changed our minds. But we plan to go visit by May, or maybe June, unless we don't. So we're grateful for all the time we get to spend with them and for their patience with our life of freedom.

My aunt and uncle have one of our very favorite free campsites.

There we have free water, electric, sewer, wifi, and cable. They even share their meals and great conversation. They're lucky we ever leave! I like to think they put that spot in just for us. They didn't, but I like to think it. It's great to catch up with all of our cousins there and the kids have a lot of fun with theirs. That's one of the few long-standing family traditions we've been able to continue, because I grew up going there and playing with my cousins. So it's been really fun to see our kids doing the same, although most of them are grown up now! Now the next generation has already begun and our grandkids will be playing together one day. But for ours, hopefully not for a long, long time still. We really love getting to spend time with them, and it's so convenient being right next door.

While we were in Virginia, Allen reconnected with his brother, who he hadn't seen for many years. We loved getting to know some more Lundys. The kids were excited to have more cousins and they hit it off instantly. We visited them a few times there, and then met them in Florida for a Lundy family vacation. We hope to have a lot more time with them soon.

I think my brother, Ryan Hamel, has figured out the best idea of all. Instead of waiting for us to visit him, he flies to us wherever we are. So he has transportation, lodging, and our wonderful company for a free vacation anywhere in the country. So far, he's met us in Arizona, Arkansas, Colorado, Florida, and Pennsylvania. We've gone hiking, climbing, sledding, ice skating on a lake, shredding (similar to white water rafting), swimming with manatees, swimming in the ocean, exploring a volcano, gawking at the Grand Canyon, driving to the top of Pike's Peak and Mount Evans, perusing Garden of the Gods, visiting the National Naval Aviation Museum, and of course lots of eating at amazing restaurants. He also experienced life on the RVstead, which you'll read more about in the unhomesteading chapter. We certainly look forward to his next visit, once we're able to tell him where we'll be at a certain point in time.

It's been great keeping in touch on social media with our friends, but it's even better when we can go visit them. We had some great fun, parked on the farms of a few different friends in Arizona, Ohio, Idaho, and Texas. The kids were able to run free and enjoy the open space, animals, and trampolines. Many of those experiences helped inspire our RVsteading adventures. The kids loved the freedom and animals, while Allen and I liked the solitude and the possibility of building whatever we wanted. We all appreciated the bonfires, fresh fruits, vegetables, and eggs, shooting days, swimming in ponds, lots of laughter, and even some hard work.

We parked in driveways of many friends' houses across the country too. We got to stay with the Harris family, very dear friends in Arkansas, who we knew from Ohio. It was wonderful to spend quality time with them, instead of settling for quick visits. And now that her kids have grown, Shannan is a travel nurse, traveling all over the country. Our paths finally crossed again and we recently got to spend time with her hiking and sight seeing in Las Vegas. We also enjoyed the generosity of and fellowship with friends from Georgia, Texas, Colorado, and Oregon. It's so nice to be able to visit, but still have the convenience of our own home parked right outside. Of course I don't think we've ever parked the RV at a friend's house, without Allen quoting Cousin Eddie's line from the classic National Lampoon's Christmas Vacation, "Don't you go falling in love with it now, because we're taking it with us when we leave here next month."[25]

We also enjoy our visits back home in Ohio, where we can see many friends at once. It's fun to catch up and reconnect with people from our last city and also the towns where Allen and I grew up. The kids prefer going to Troy, where we launched from, to see their old friends and we try to do that at least every few years. They still enjoy the trips to our hometowns of Waverly and Peebles, though, and listening to our stories from childhood. They especially like the favorite pizza places we always visit.

We took them to their first high school football game and their reactions were so amusing. They were shocked at the real emotion from the Waverly Tiger team. They had no idea how strongly the students, or the community, felt about high school sports.

They said the players were intense, the parents were more intense, and even the grandparents were going crazy. Remember, to them, a game is just a game, played for fun. I remember being in that mindset in high school, so I identified with the fans. But I've also undone my thinking and have a whole new perspective too. It was funny to watch our kids experience a typical Midwestern Friday night, and find it very odd. To people who love that way of life, like I once did, that might sound sad. They may think our kids are missing out. But to our family, who prefers a wider variety of experiences across the country, once was enough. I asked the kids what they thought about the game and what they were missing. They all agreed they'd probably enjoy it, if they went to a school, but they'd rather not have to do the same thing week after week.

The kids were also amazed at how quickly news spread among friends in our small town. Last year we went back to Waverly during the summer for Allen's softball team reunion. We camped nearby and tried to see as many people as we could. The first night, we went to a softball practice, where Allen just barely missed making a diving catch. The next morning, at a parade in town, someone who wasn't even there greeted Allen and said he heard he almost made a diving catch. The kids couldn't believe it and talked about that all week! They were amazed he didn't even make the catch, and it was still news. Of course similar things happened for the rest of our visit, because it's a small town.

They were also surprised we knew people everywhere we went. Restaurants, stores, churches, parades, games, and even driving down the road, we saw so many old friends. The kids are used to getting to know others in a campground, but they haven't lived in a small town where everyone knows everyone. It was a great visit and we managed to see many more friends than usual. Being there during the Heritage Days softball tournament, where Allen and I met, made it extra special. It was fun to visit friends and to share it all with our kids.

So we've been able to stay in contact with our friends, reconnect with old friends, and connect with more new friends than we ever imagined. We were worried about losing friends, but we found even more, thanks to the trailblazer tribe. We have been sad as we parted ways with friends, but we also knew we'd see them down the road. We haven't resisted making friends, because the heartbreak isn't so bad, knowing we'll see them later. Our kids have had an unending supply of playmates and have plenty of best friends. And we're able to reconnect with old friends on our trips back home too. We didn't end up unfriending at all, just rethinking everything about friendship. While stepping out into the unknown, we knew things wouldn't be the same, but we discovered they were even better.

CHAPTER 8: UNCHURCHING

In case you haven't caught on from the other chapters, and because I don't want you to be angry about the word unchurching, let me be clear from the start. I don't hate God and I don't hate church. Our family loves God and His church, so rest easy. Unchurching does not mean not going to church or not liking church. Remember, unschooling does not mean not learning, and unworking does not mean not working. Similarly, unchurching just means undoing what you think about church. So, if the word bothered you, hopefully you can sigh in relief and read the rest with an open, less angry, mind.

Because I want to be sure, let's start with a positive tone from the beginning. My friend Deny Lemaster, a minister in Missouri, posted this on social media recently. "My son called me early this morning from his home two states away and we talked for an hour. Now I know how God feels when I pray."[26] That's beautiful, isn't it? That is simply undoing what you think about prayer. See? It's not scary and you're not mad at me. Let's continue with that!

Before I share why we even began undoing what we thought about church, let me explain how it started. When we hit the road, we were able to take most of the important things with us. We took our jobs, school, hobbies, and even our friends in a sense. But one thing we had to leave behind was our church community. We didn't have a plan for this, it was just another unknown.

When we started planning, we assumed we would visit churches along the way. We were looking forward to just enjoying the services without feeling the need to evaluate everything as we do when we move to a new town. We would not be church shopping. We also would not be plugging in, since we would be moving on. So we wouldn't need to worry about the size, the fit, the programs, the opportunities, or even the beliefs very much, as we would only attend once. So as long as it was a Bible teaching church, we might visit. We looked forward to exposing the kids to the wide range of churches in the USA, including big, small, lively, serious, formal, informal, traditional, charismatic, etc. If we were settling down, we would be extremely picky, but on the road, we looked forward to enjoying the variety. We knew the methods would be different, but the message would be the same. While Allen would miss playing drums and guitar and we all would miss our Grace friends very much, we were excited about our church visits across the country.

When we hit the road, we started doing just that. We attended a local church wherever we were. I would usually research online to make sure they were at least Bible-based. Most were, but not all. Of course not all even had websites, so often we just guessed. Quite a few times, we chose churches with the word grace in the name, just because it reminded us of home. But we did indeed get the variety we'd hoped for. I often alternated styles too. If we went to a big church with a band one week, we went to a small non-instrumental one then next. Since we were changing states too, the culture was different as well. It was quite fascinating observing all the similarities and differences.

Sometimes there were friendly faces, and sometimes there weren't. Sometimes we felt warmly welcomed, and sometimes we were ignored. Sometimes we felt awkwardly welcomed as we had to stand, raise our hands, or tell everyone where we were from. You know the unspoken, but understood, "assigned seats" you find in many smaller, older churches? We'd always hoped not to ruin someone's day by displacing them, but we did hear a few grumbles. Once though, we learned how serious people can be about their spots on their pews. A lady started to sit on Matt! He was seven, so not very hard to miss. Our family took up five seats on the left of what we hoped was a friendly pew. Two people sat to our right, without a glance in our direction, filling the short pew. A third lady started making her way past the two and I thought maybe she was coming to greet us, because there was certainly no room. So I looked up and smiled, but she didn't even look at us. She just turned around to sit on top of Matt! I jerked him out of the way quickly onto my lap. We were both dumbfounded. He was almost smashed by a church lady's bum! I'd have understood asking us to squeeze down. I'd even have understood asking us to sit somewhere else. But to sit on a child, that was just the strangest experience. The rest of the family squeezed over to let Matt sit, but I stayed between the lady and him. That wasn't a greet-your-neighbor type church, so we never even spoke to her, which was probably for the best. Obviously we wouldn't judge that, or any other, church by one person's behavior, but it was an interesting encounter.

We also found it quite convenient, when traveling on a Saturday, to park in a church parking lot at night and attend services the next morning. It's certainly easy to make it to church on time when it is in your front yard! Sometimes we showed up underdressed and sometimes we were overdressed. Sometimes it seemed to matter and sometimes it didn't. Sometimes we felt invisible, but other times we were invited to share meals and conversations. Once we were invited to a church reunion at a nearby camp, where we were treated like part of the family. Frequently, we felt like we stepped backwards in time fifty years. Occasionally, we felt like we were transported into the future with all the lights and lasers. Sometimes there was dancing in the aisles, while other times it felt more like a funeral. We found contemporary and traditional services we enjoyed and we also found contemporary and traditional services we didn't. We heard meaningful messages and questionable ones in big and small churches alike. Once we were surrounded by cult-like chanting, claiming monetary gain from unclaimed funds and insurance payouts. That one we left early, because it got even stranger, discussing drama and chastising members. So again, it was just fascinating to see the many differences.

We experienced a very good sampling of church life across America, in my opinion. And while we tried to remain open-minded and non-judgmental, we found ourselves beginning to judge and compare. We weren't looking for the perfect fit, but we were starting to pick apart what we liked and what we didn't. Comparing notes with each other and the kids, we were really evaluating churches on their programming and presentation. We were like uninvited secret shoppers who swooped into appraise a church, with no end goal in mind.

One particular Sunday morning, we started to realize something big. On the way out of a large church, Allen and I agreed it was great. We had enjoyed worshiping, the band was rocking, and the message was interesting. When we picked up the kids, they were very excited. As usual, we asked how their class time was and they said it was awesome. As Allen quizzed them more, we realized they were just pumped about the candy they ate and the games they played. The children's area was very cheerful, with colorful murals displayed around an impressive tree house playground in the center. I'm sure they had a Bible lesson of some sort, but it didn't stick with any of our kids.

We saw it very plainly the kids only liked a church for the entertainment value. If they were entertained, it was great. If they were bored, it wasn't great. This really struck Allen and me as pivotal, and we wanted them to look at church differently. That's when it hit us. We were doing the very same thing. If there was a talented band, familiar songs we liked, or a captivating speaker, it was great. If we were bored, it wasn't great. In other words, we only liked a church for the entertainment value too.

Honestly, that really stung. We wanted to worship God across the country, experiencing different church communities. But we ended up judging the methods and motives of a community we weren't even a part of. And we were teaching our young children to do the same. Where was God in all this? Well, we pretty much took that role upon ourselves, and not very effectively either. He was probably shaking His head, waiting for us to realize the path we were on.

So we took a step back and decided to undo our thinking. We prayed, read, thought, studied, and talked to others on the same journey. We should have expected the trailblazers. They were experiencing the same things. We all realized going to a church, when you are not a part of that church community, is very different from going to a church when you are. If you are always a visitor, you are missing the main point of church – the community. We grew up in church and knew what to expect, but only from the perspective of people who knew what to expect. It took us stepping outside our box to even consider looking at things differently.

As we looked around at other traveling families, we found a wide range of practices around the idea of church. Some took church on the road, attempting to recreate everything they left. Some watched their home church online, but still lacked the community. Some tried to fill that hole with acts of service, while some found great freedom in serving others. Those two might sound the same, but they are very different. Some faithfully visited different places every week. Some visited until they became disillusioned or at least had changes in perspective. Some stopped going at all. All were asking the same question, though they often didn't know what the question was. I believe it started as, "How can we be a part of God's church on the road?" But as most of us found that to be almost impossible, I think it shifted to, "What is God's church anyway?"

If you grew up in church, just admit it. "We are the church!" popped into your head. That's preached from the pulpit and amen'd from the seats. Then backs are patted, seats are emptied, and that phrase is forgotten until the next time. Now, don't get fired up. Maybe you are the church. Maybe you have this thing figured out. I'd love to hear more if so. But don't forget I sat in those seats. So did Allen. So did hundreds of our traveling friends. And most of us still don't understand being the church. When you hear, "What time is church?" No one says, "Well, I am the church, so right now." "Where is your church?" is never answered "Right here, since it's me." You can serve others, give to charity, invite people to church, share Christ, and make moral decisions, but those are things you do. How do you be?

In general conversation, the word church means the building or service in the building. In more specific discussions, more of us understand that yes, the church refers to the community which meets in that building. But if you are a nomad trying to understand being the church without access to the building, the service, or the community, that is just confusing.

Our life simply did not fit into our current view of church. But surely there had to be an option for travelers. We just could not imagine God saying "Nope. If you want to worship me, you have to give up your nomadic ways. Then you have to find a specific building and I'll meet you there." That sounds curiously like something from the Old Testament.

In undoing our thinking about church, and the way it has always been from our perspective, we tried to go back to the beginning. Looking at how Jesus described the church, and comparing that to the church we see today, was actually disturbing. Especially since we were trying to uncover what it should be, instead of just accepting how it's always been. Furthermore, if we did manage to discover the exact intentions, the precise answer to everything, the problem would remain that today's church is how it is. We still couldn't fit in. We couldn't sit down and convince everyone else to reprogram their thinking. We were only willing to do so because we had no other choice.

As a reminder, I am not an expert. This is not a theological investigation into the words of Christ. Both of those things should be quite obvious, but I want to make it very clear, because we found far more questions than answers. This quote by Wayne Jacobsen helped me feel a little better about my lack of understanding, though. "If you share my frustration with the disparity between the church as Scripture talks about her and what we see reflected in our religious institutions, you're not alone. You're standing in a long line that includes the likes of Francis of Assisi, John Wycliffe, Martin Luther, John Wesley, and nameless others who dared to ask the difficult questions and struggled with the uncomfortable answers."[27]

So we prayed, read, thought, and studied more. And we talked to more trailblazers searching for answers. We didn't find the answers though, and Jacobsen explained why. "Our underlying assumption is that there must be a formula we can follow to replicate church whenever we want. Wouldn't you think if such a model existed, Jesus would have shared it with us? As long as we are seeking to implement a model, we are not following him."[27] We were indeed looking for a model we could fit our nomadic life into.

I know, you want to scream, "Hebrews 10:25 says not to give up meeting together!" I said it too, for years, as we tried to figure out how not to give up meeting together. It's the Bible, so of course I agree. And we do still meet together often with believers. But it doesn't say not to give up going to church on Sunday. I assumed it did. But if you read more, you see the chapter before it is all about the tabernacle, sacrifices, and priests. Then the beginning of this chapter is about how Christ is the high priest, how he fulfilled those sacrifices, and how we can boldly enter the holiest place by a new and living way. So the whole point of the two chapters is that type of church meeting is no longer necessary. It does mention gathering, love, good deeds, and encouragement, as do other often misunderstood verses. That sounds like a community, but it doesn't require a church service.

We started thinking maybe God was serious about the whole two most important commandments, love God and love others. Could it be that easy though? Could we be the church, by simply being part of a community who loves God and people? Wherever we were, could we engage in the community He was building around us, instead of a community who met in a building? Jacobsen seemed to do just that. "By simply following what Jesus put on my heart and loving people around me, I found myself living squarely in the middle of the church life I had been hungering for all those years."[27] This unchurching idea was very appealing!

I'll admit that felt way too simple. It was too different. It also seemed to make sense. But we couldn't "do nothing," right? There had to be more to it. This got me thinking about a lesson about God our daughter taught us years ago. Lizzy came to us at six-years-old and, understandably, brought some baggage with her. Because of her past, she was afraid of rejection and aimed for perfection. All we wanted was for her to love us and let us love her. But she was so busy anxiously trying to do this, don't do that, say this, and don't say that, all to be perfect enough for us to not send her away. We simply wanted her to relax and just be. Lizzy didn't trust that, though, and tried to earn it. It struck us that God wants the same thing, for us to just be. Love Him and let Him love us. Sometimes we don't trust that and also try to earn it. I felt like that's what we were trying to do with church.

So we tried to relax and just be. We looked at the community around us with a new perspective. We also engaged with a wider community, including local residents, our nomadic friends currently close to us, and our online community. We found something very different, but very meaningful. We had real conversations around so many campfires which were more authentic than any we ever had in churches. We found so many others who were searching for that community and finding it too. The tribe of trailblazers gathered and it was beautiful.

When we gathered, we certainly shared love, good deeds, and encouragement. We also shared meals, rides, music, teaching, laughter, and so much more. Many conversations with other RVers started with a simple question about church. They would say, "You know, we've been rethinking that lately." They would become a part of the tribe. It felt real and it felt right. Sometimes we would still struggle with feeling like we weren't doing enough. We weren't checking off a list. And it wasn't easy to communicate this perspective shift to our kids. But then we would have a wonderful conversation or a spontaneous worship session with another family. It would remind us that God said He would be with us when two or three are gathered.

Sometimes we still go to church services. We just take our new perspectives and leave our judgmental attitudes. Sometimes we worship there and sometimes we worship in nature. Not everybody gets it, and that's okay. I recently posted a beautiful picture of the mountains we were enjoying, with a caption which read "This is where we worship." I could tell people didn't understand, because they started sharing church suggestions. While those were kind gestures, our worship had nothing to do with a church. Just like church, worship sometimes becomes a word that doesn't mean worship at all. You can certainly worship in a church, and sometimes we do, but that day we chose to worship in the mountains. We always feel closest to God there, so it makes sense. Unchurching didn't mean giving up on church or God. It actually meant finding both in more places.

So we have a better grasp on church and our lifestyle does fit into it now. Our traveling life forced us to think outside the box, but it also allowed us to. What felt like a negative at first turned into a positive, because we have a much better understanding of what it means to be a part of God's church. We had to undo our thinking, but it was so worth it. Unchurching, like so many other things we had to rethink, turned out to be much better than we imagined.

CHAPTER 9: UNPLUGGING

When most people think of RVing, they probably think of a motor home or a towed camper rolling down the highway, then stopping to plug in at a campground. That's what I think of. I do love being plugged in. It's pretty convenient to have unlimited electric, water, and sewer we don't have to maintain or pay for. And it's very nice to soak in a hot tub you don't have to clean or work out in a gym you don't have to equip. Of course campgrounds also provide friends for campfires and often lots of entertainment. But sometimes the neighbors are too close and too plentiful. Sometimes the rules and crowds are tiresome. Sometimes there are no other kids, and sometimes there are too many. Sometimes our family's sarcastic comments are misunderstood by people walking by our open windows. Sometimes it's nice to just unplug.

We love getting off the grid and camping on public land out in the middle of nowhere. That is freedom. Camping in an RV with no hook-ups is called boondocking or dry camping, and it's glorious. We can't do it forever though, because we need those utilities. Electricity doesn't fall from the sky, unless of course you have solar power. And water doesn't fall from the sky. Well, it does, but you can't direct it into your tank, unless of course you have a collection system. So yes, actually many RVers have these setups and can boondock forever! We don't though, so like many parts of our journey, we go about things a little less traditionally.

If we're careful with our water usage, we can stay unplugged for about ten days. We prefer to boondock for about a week, though. Then we're all pretty ready to have all the conveniences again. I will admit we are spoiled. We may live in an RV, but we are not campers. I laugh when people think we're always roughing it. We rarely rough it. Even when we're boondocking, we have everything we need, plus everything we don't. We have satellite TV. Matt has his Xbox. We have a Keurig coffee station with all the flavored syrups for our lattes. I use my Instant Pot and convection oven as always. I might start to use the microwave and realize the generator's not on, so I have to go start it. Okay, I have to send a kid to go start it. So it does take about thirty seconds out of my day, but I'm never in a hurry anyway. Not much changes for us when we're boondocking. If you have no interest in RVing or boondocking, keep reading just for the stories. If you do, though, also keep reading. Basically never stop reading this book. You're almost finished anyway!

Some RVers love boondocking and have impressive setups. If you're interested in spending a lot of time off the grid, they will become your tribe. They love the freedom of not depending on campgrounds, plus the beauty and solitude of unplugging. They can teach you all about solar power, water collection, potable water, sewer macerators, composting toilets, wood heat, convenience stations, outdoor showers, public land, and more. We know many of these RVers who crave this freedom and never pay for campgrounds. They are the experts.

We're definitely not experts, but I will share how we make it work. I don't want to be your instructor, because I want much better for you. There are amazing trailblazers out there who will instruct and advise. I just want to be your example of the simplicity of unplugging, because if I can do it, anyone can. You don't have to overthink boondocking, but you might have to undo what you think about it now.

Like most things, we keep it very simple. You don't have to know all the things above to unplug. You don't have to invest, remodel, research, and install every possible gadget. You don't have to go off the grid for months or weeks at a time. You don't even have to go off the grid. You could just walk outside and unplug your rig. I honestly couldn't tell you how, because I've never done it. Listen, Allen and I agreed nine years ago I would take care of the inside and he would take care of the outside. That has worked perfectly for all this time, so don't judge. So go unplug, or send a kid to unplug. Now you are boondocking. Great job!

Our boondocking setup consists of a generator and that's pretty much it. Most every RV will have the rest, which is a battery, a propane tank, and a water tank. That's really all there is to it. That's all we need to unplug, and still be comfortable, for a few nights during travel or a week of fun in the middle of nowhere.

We just have one battery. Some boondockers connect a whole bank of them for more power. Our RV battery will run the lights, furnace blower, and water pump. We have two forty pound propane tanks. Propane will run the refrigerator, stove, and furnace. Our water tank can hold forty gallons of water, though many RVs hold up to one hundred. But forty is enough for our family of five for ten days. If we're traveling, Allen only likes to bring a third of a tank of water. That provides us with enough for a few days, without adding a lot of weight. If we need something that is plugged into an outlet, like the coffeemaker, microwave, or TV, then we need to run the generator. Can one actually need a TV? I'm not sure about that, but if we want the TV, we have to generate.

We don't have solar power at all. We just haven't needed it enough to bother installing it. We have a generator to supply our power. Specifically, it's a Honda 3000-watt inverter generator. Because it's a Honda, it's quiet too. So it's not like the giant, loud ones you see for houses. You generally can't hear it from the next site over. You might if you park super close to us, but you shouldn't do that anyway. People seem to like doing that to us lately, but it's not cool. Anyway, according to Allen, we use about seven gallons of gasoline for a week of boondocking. Again, I wouldn't know because that's an outside job. But I do know in Nevada, that currently means less than $19 for a week of freedom, without roughing it.

We get a lot of practice boondocking when we're on the road. We usually don't have long travel days, but sometimes we have a plan that takes us a few days to reach our destination. We never stop at campgrounds on the way. That would be such an inconvenience to find, reserve, pay, check in, back in, hook up, and slide out just for one night. Plus, then you have to slide in, unhook, and pull out the next day. We've met a few families who travel that way and I just can't fathom it. Of course they often have routes and stops planned more precisely than our winging it in a general direction. But we just stop at a rest area, truck stop, Walmart, or other parking spot we see on the road or find on one of the many RV parking apps. Walmart is a frequent choice, because we can do our grocery shopping too. On lazy nights, we rent a Redbox movie and buy rotisserie chicken and a few side dishes. I love dinner and a movie with no effort! Usually though, I have an easy dinner prepared and we watch a movie online or on the DVR. So, it still doesn't require much effort.

So we're unplugged for the night. We usually park and run the generator long enough for dinner and a movie. That gives our phones and laptops time to charge fully as well. After that, we turn it off and play card games, go shopping, or go to bed. In the morning, we generate long enough to make coffee. In full disclosure, Allen generates, makes coffee, gets a little work done, and then drags the rest of us out of bed. We may be in a parking lot, but we're also in our cozy beds after a normal night's sleep. We're also not morning people. When we finally emerge, we all get ready, eat breakfast, brush our teeth, and hit the road.

We've practiced a lot on the road, but unplugging for a week isn't much different really. We run the generator in the morning for coffee and breakfast, then again in the evening for dinner and TV. We might need it for a few minutes at lunch, if we need the microwave or toaster. During the daytime though, we usually don't need power. We're often gone hiking or climbing anyway. If not, we may be working on our laptops or phones. Or we may be playing card games. Sometimes the kids like to just sit around complaining about how bored they are. That's great fun for everyone. Of course they do that in the campgrounds too.

We are pretty careful and try to conserve water. Allen likes to kindly remind us all, by yelling "Trickle!" each time we wash our hands or rinse a cup. That's become our family mantra when unplugged. In his defense though, we do tend to forget. And it's a pain if we run out of water before the week is over. So we trickle when washing up, rinsing dishes, or brushing our teeth. We take military showers if we must, or wait to get back to a campground. If you're not familiar with that term, it just means rinsing quickly, then turning the water off to soap up, then rinsing off. We often bring jugs of drinking water, just to help the water in the tank last longer. We use paper plates and coffee cups, for easier cleanup. I usually plan easier meals which won't make big messes. Sometimes I cook a bunch of ground turkey and shredded chicken ahead of time, so we can use that all week and save time and dishes. A bagged salad with reheated meat makes a quick and easy dinner. Sometimes though, I'm just in the mood for spaghetti squash lasagna, which means I use the Instant Pot, a glass bowl, and a casserole dish. We try to keep the dishes minimal though. We usually only have to wash dishes once or twice a week and of course, we use as little water as possible.

We also conserve power, by keeping the lights off when possible. And we conserve gasoline, by turning the generator off as soon as we no longer need it. That's really it. Boondocking doesn't have to be very complicated. Not much changes when we're unplugged, except we're a little more careful with water and power. There are groups dedicated to all things boondocking and, if that's your jam, you will love the guidance available. We just like to keep things simple and find it to be pretty easy. And most importantly, we love the freedom it gives us.

We're very comfortable being unplugged for about a week, but we've found places so amazing we had to stay longer. We stayed for a whole month in a beautiful area of Colorado. Buena Vista is a picturesque little mountain town with endless whitewater kayaking and climbing. There is a whitewater park in the middle of the town. There are places to sit all along the Arkansas River, to watch kayakers playing at the rapids. There is rock climbing everywhere. The routes are easy to access and have breathtaking views. There is also plenty of hiking, browsing charming local shops, and taking scenic mountain drives. On top of all that, quite literally, is the free camping. More than 100,000 acres of public land overlook Buena Vista and the Arkansas Valley, with the Collegiate Peaks as a stunning mountain backdrop. It's one of the most magnificent views we've seen in the entire country, and it's framed in our window.

Since we weren't ready to leave this amazing area after a week, we had to figure out a few things. We were out of water and our tanks were getting full. Some boondockers have portable tanks to take waste to a dump and other tanks to bring potable water back. We don't want to make room to store all of the equipment, so we just packed up the rig and headed to a campground. We paid a fee to use their convenience station to dump and fill the tanks. Then we headed back up to our campsite. Sadly, another RV had claimed our spot, so we had to find a different one. Fortunately, the spot just down the road had an even better view!

We also needed some longer showers and found some pay showers at a park in town. Since it's a kayaker town, it's geared toward the outdoor camping types. The local laundromat, which we needed to visit after a week anyway, also had showers. Another park had a water refill station, so it was convenient for refilling our jugs for drinking water. So we were able to stay for a month this way, visiting the campground every ten days or so, utilizing the public showers, and refilling our water jugs in town. We stayed until it was just too cold for us. Colorado in September at a high elevation is pretty iffy for the Lundys.

Because we don't mind boondocking, we've been able to stay at some really fun places. We found an apple orchard and farm near Salt Lake City where we could park for a weekend. They made fresh apple cider and it was so good. We were there during a fall festival, so they had a bouncy house, face painting, apple cider donuts, and hay rides. They played a movie on the side of a truck at night. The kids loved playing on the playground and the bouncy house. And we all loved the fresh cider and donuts!

Antelope Island in Salt Lake City was incredible and unexpected. We were just looking for an inexpensive few days of downtime before a work event. We found a cheap campground on Antelope Island and it turned into a great stay. It was a primitive site, meaning no hookups, so we had to boondock. But we had a private campsite, on the Great Salt Lake, with bison grazing nearby! The kids dug in the sand right outside, played down by the lake, and had a ball. As a state park, they even had a Junior Ranger program. So we all learned about the salty lake and the only things that can live in it (brine flies and brine shrimp). There were bison and antelope everywhere! We visited a historical ranch where we learned more of the history of the island, and saw old buildings, equipment, horses, coyotes, and a horned owl. It was fascinating.

In the Florida Everglades, we boondocked at a lake with the alligators. And I do mean with them. The alligators are everywhere down there, including in the campgrounds. They were in the lake, on the banks, and right outside our window. Yes, we had to keep a close eye on Jack, and on the kids when it was time to walk Jack. We laughed as an RV was attempting to pull into the next campsite. They had to wait a while, because an alligator was there and refused to move. They were amused, too, and didn't mind waiting their turn.

Unplugging helped us to spend an entire winter in Arizona for free. We have a membership campground near Sedona which allows us to stay for three weeks for free. But then we have to go somewhere else for a week, before we can return. Usually we just go to another membership campground, but there isn't another one in this area. Fortunately, there is public land right across from the campground! So at the end of each three week period, we just drove across the street and boondocked for a week. That spot was very convenient, because we could drive back into the campground to do laundry, take showers, and visit friends. Plus, it was surrounded by great mountain views of Sedona!

We had a lovely free campsite on public land in the Hoh Rainforest in Washington. It was a gorgeous spot along the Hoh River, which was a beautiful aquamarine. If you're a Saturday Night Live or Chris Farley fan, you'll understand why we always get a kick out of saying we live in a van down by the river! Allen took the kids on an overnight backpacking trip through the rainforest while I stayed home to work and hold down the fort. Allen and

Josh also paddled twelve miles down the scenic river in kayaks. It was such a pretty area and so strange to see a rainforest in the Unites States.

We spent a fun week boondocking with the Johnson family in Kanab, Utah. Can you tell we've had a lot of fun with them? We toured Arizona and Utah together, mostly staying in campgrounds. But we wanted some time off the grid and we circled our RVs and trucks around a shade tree for a cool campsite. We enjoyed some geocaching, shooting, and hiking. Because it was public land, many people brought off-road vehicles and horses. It was really neat to see them before they hit the trails.

Some of our favorite boondocking sites are located just outside of Las Vegas, Nevada. The Lake Mead National Recreation Area has multiple roads with tons of free campsites available. It's a popular area and can get very busy, but most of the sites aren't too close together. So you can still enjoy the beautiful views of the lake and mountains. We also love the Desert National Wildlife Refuge, northwest of Las Vegas. There are only three sites available there, so it feels much more secluded. There are lovely mountain views all around, miles of open space, and many hidden gems in the refuge. We love being camped near Las Vegas, without all the lights, noise, and traffic. While the city can be fun, we really love climbing in Red Rock Canyon. So unplugging and camping for free in this area is just about perfect.

Sometimes we're not technically camping, but we're still able to take advantage of boondocking. When we visit amusement parks, we bring the RV with us. It's so nice to be able to take a break and come back to our home in the parking lot to fix a good meal or take a nap. We can also change clothes if it's too hot or cold or if we're too wet from a water ride. We can schedule a video call or attend an online training if we need to work a little that day as well. Then we can head back in to the park until it closes. We usually spend the night in a nearby parking lot and come right back in the morning. It's certainly handy to take your home with you everywhere you go!

Unplugging doesn't have to be overwhelming or difficult at all.

It's quite convenient and peaceful. And it's definitely worth the feeling of freedom it brings. We've learned a lot from the trailblazer tribe. Even though we don't really need most of the tips to extend our boondocking, it's great to know they're there if we ever do. If you've considered unplugging, but haven't had the courage yet, I hope you'll give it a try. If you have no desire, I think you might be missing out, but isn't it cool you don't have to? Personally, I love the freedom of being completely alone, in the middle of nowhere, with just our little home. It's especially fun when we're also watching a movie via satellite, after eating a yummy meal, and enjoying our fancy lattes. We have all the conveniences of home, even though we're unplugged. That's not roughing it at all.

CHAPTER 10: UNHOMESTEADING

One glorious part of our nomadic life of freedom is not having a yard, but guess what we started missing a little bit after a few years of travel? The freedom of having a yard! We didn't miss the responsibility of maintaining it or the time and effort involved. We stayed in campgrounds, on public lands, and even in friends' driveways, and it was nice to just drive off to the next stop with no cares left behind. Like I said in the unplugging chapter, though, sometimes we just wanted a break from the campgrounds. But unlike boondocking, sometimes we wanted to have the freedom of being unplugged, but still have the conveniences of being plugged in. Sometimes we wanted a place where we could do whatever we wanted without worrying about neighbors, rules, etiquette, or judgment. Sometimes, for whatever reason, Matt just wanted to run around in his underwear. Seriously, he was eleven and very set on the idea of having the freedom to run around in his skivvies with no one to see or care. We honestly don't know where this came from. We didn't encourage it, but that was his goal.

So we began to search for the perfect campground away from campground. We just wanted some hunting land originally. Allen wanted a place to hunt in the spring and fall and we would continue to travel and explore in the summer and winter. We wanted the views and isolation of the mountains, but of course it had to be RV accessible too. We finally settled on Idaho and headed west. When we got there, though, we changed our minds. Idaho is gorgeous and definitely a great area, but it was so far away from the grandparents in Florida, and pretty much everything else in the country. Something in the center of the US would be best, but the mountains we wanted were out west. Arkansas kept popping up in our searches and we had quickly dismissed it, because the mountains weren't big enough. After talking to some friends about the hunting there and seeing the ridiculously low prices, though, we considered it. The mountains weren't as high, but they were still mountains, with great views and possibilities. The more we learned about the Ozarks, the more interested we became.

So we headed southeast to Arkansas to continue the search. And there we found what had to be the perfect location on top of a mountain in the Ozarks. It was very isolated, with great views, trees, fields, and woods. It was a mile from our own little beach on Bull Shoals Lake. The lake was surrounded by public land, which meant more hunting areas. There was a good dirt road off a county highway, and a level spot for the RV with a well, electricity, and a septic system. It had great cell service and satellite reception, and, of all things, DSL internet. There were a few families spread over miles of mountains, so there were neighbors if needed, but plenty of space of our own. We even found another family, on top of the next mountain, who used to RV and also had adopted children, so we hit it off and our kids had friends. It was pretty much everything we could have wanted and more. And they were almost giving away these eleven perfect acres, so we paid for it with cash. We named it Lundy Mountain.

We cleared the land, fought (and lost) a battle against chiggers, and put in two RV sites with full hookups. The chiggers were pretty traumatic for all of us. We finally recovered and learned to avoid them. But to this day, if you mention nail polish as a remedy to anyone in our family, you might get cut. I said it was traumatic. We got a trampoline, because we promised the kids when we hit the road that would be the first thing we bought if we ever had land. They spent hours on that thing again and it was fun to see them so happy. And yes, Matt did indeed get to run around in his underwear. Once again, we didn't encourage it, but he reached his goal. He waited for a rainy day and ran joyfully through the field in his undies. I took pictures from inside, because he was so happy and free. Unless that would be weird, then of course I didn't do that at all.

After getting everything set up, it was time to make it a hunting camp. Allen and the boys found some great hunting spots and started bringing home squirrels and deer. Even Lizzy bagged a squirrel! We learned all about processing our own meat and worked out a great system. With all five of us doing our parts, we had a deer processed and in the freezer in less than an hour. I found great recipes and we enjoyed a lot of free, organic, free-range, acorn-fed venison. We had to buy a second freezer for the RV to hold it all. We enjoyed a great fall, but as soon as it got cold, we pulled in the slides and headed to Florida.

When we came back in the spring, we planned more of the same, except Allen had other ideas. Each time we visited our neighbors, who were homesteaders, he was so fascinated. It did look fun though, and we were definitely interested in being even more self-sufficient. So, after four years of RVing adventures, we added even more by RVsteading! Yes, we were homesteading in an RV. Like most everything we do, it wasn't very traditional, so I call it unhomesteading.

Wikipedia says homesteading is "a lifestyle of self-sufficiency. It is characterized by subsistence agriculture, home preservation of foodstuffs..."[28] In our self-contained RV, we are pretty self-sufficient as far as providing our own power and water. And we have everything we need to cook, clean, work, sleep, etc. Then we found Lundy Mountain and had been living off the land as much as the hunting and fishing allowed. But we had been thinking about gardening, fruit trees, fresh milk and eggs, and really providing all of our needs. So visiting our neighbors' homestead with lots of animals sent us over the edge!

We loved our mountain and already had the home, so we just needed the stead. We also loved the RV life still, and we didn't want to give it up. So we didn't build a house with a pantry, cellar, and all the amenities you generally have on a homestead. We didn't want to be tied down. We did build a barn with a chicken coop, goat pen, greenhouse, and summer kitchen. We also put in a garden and fruit trees. But we designed everything so we could leave anytime, most likely at the first sign of snow. Our first year of unhomesteading was really fun and we learned so much.

Life in the mountains was always new and interesting. Unschooling went to a new level for all of us as we learned everything together. Of course the trailblazers gathered around to help. They were on the next mountain, down the road, on a farm, at the feed store, at the hardware store, at the archery shop, and pretty much everywhere we looked. Northern Arkansas had the same slow pace of our intentionally peaceful life. No one was in a hurry, so people were happy to stop and chat for a few minutes or a few hours. It felt like the whole state had that laid-back RV campground vibe. Everywhere we went, we were surrounded by the homesteader, prepper, survivalist, and completely awesome type of people who loved to help others. They were self-sufficient, independent, loners, who were perfectly happy on their own, but even more happy to help these newbies.

It had the small town feel, without the small town gossip and drama. Of course we weren't even in a small town. To give you an idea of the remoteness, it was a slow, curvy, twenty minute drive to the nearest town, which had two hundred people. It was a slower, curvier, forty-five minute drive to the nearest "big" city, which had thirteen thousand people. So we were really on our own, except for the tribe of trailblazers. They helped us learn about chickens, ducks, turkeys, rabbits, and goats, plus gardening, canning, foraging, and just surviving on the mountain.

The tribe didn't just give advice either. They worked with us and each other, using a bartering system. We traded homemade bread for goat milk with one neighbor and chickens for eggs with another. Our goats were too young for milk and our chickens too young to lay eggs, but we were able to help our neighbors and benefit from their homesteads as well.

We see a lot of helpful cooperation within campgrounds too. It's not uncommon to see someone loan their only truck to strangers, spend hours fixing a mechanical issue, or offer to babysit so new friends can have a rare date night. We've been on the giving and receiving end of much kindness over the last nine years in our campground and homesteading communities. Maybe it's that friendly Arkansas/RV vibe, but it's a beautiful thing to experience. Maybe you have that in your neighborhood already. If not, why not? Is that just the way it's always been? Maybe by undoing what you think, you could be the one to start it.

Continuing with our unschooling, all five of us became life learning, farming, gardening, unhomesteading students. We learned the hard way how to live off the land on the top of Lundy Mountain in Arkansas. We all helped build the barn and animal pens. We learned how to raise baby goats, which was ridiculously fun. We figured out putting in a garden on top of rock was quite challenging. We found enjoying the fruits (and vegetables) of our labor was pretty nice though. We built a greenhouse with a water collection system. We learned quite a bit about the birthing process too, thanks to the rabbits. What an education that was, especially for our adopted kids who haven't had much exposure to birth and babies. Even Jack, our chicken and rabbit eating dog, learned which animals he wasn't allowed to eat! It was so fun to watch the kids and animals all enjoying the land. It really was a wonderful experience, learning in our mountaintop classroom.

One funny lesson the kids quickly learned was "always check your shoes." And that was brought about by them forgetting the lesson of the day before, which was "don't leave your shoes outside." We found out the tarantulas in Arkansas were huge and they liked to hide in shoes!

Another lesson was something they didn't tell us at the chicken store. Apparently good chicken owners already knew this. You have to wipe the adorable little chicks' rear ends! Pasted vent, also called pasty butt, is exactly as disgusting as it sounds. It was a dirty job, and certainly not one I would have ever envisioned. But it was necessary for raising healthy chicks, so we just did it. Well, I didn't do it. That's what we had children for.

The chickens brought many other challenges, like keeping them safe from Jack. He has a sordid history with chickens, so we knew it would take some work. He learned very quickly, though, and ended up being a great chicken guard dog! It probably helped that we started with tiny chicks, because he was afraid of them.

Jack is strange that way. Human babies scare him too. But he learned to hang out with the chickens, ignore their antics, and watch for trouble. And sometimes he would steal their food. He was a great chicken guard dog, not a perfect one. One day we watched him sneak over to a group of chicks who were gathered in a big circle. We assumed he was going for their food. But he broke up the crowd, chasing them off, and then gently nudged a little chick that wasn't able to get up! We didn't know what was wrong with it, or why they were all on top of it, but it was finally able to stand, walk around, and eat. We were quite shocked and of course proud. Our chicken killer turned into a chicken protector.

Besides our animal care, lessons in survival were also common of course. Lizzy and I often came home from the store to find Allen and the boys immersed in some survival class. I think Allen just waited until I left, which didn't happen often since the city was so far away. We would find them drinking staghorn sumac lemonade, made from trees on the mountain. No, this isn't the poison sumac, so don't fret. They would be pulling weeds like plantains, not for lawn maintenance, but for salads. Or they would be roasting squirrels on sticks over the fire. Sometimes it was grasshoppers instead. Believe it or not, they taste like chicken. Are you surprised I tried them? I did my fair share of things I never thought I would do on that mountain. Grasshoppertizers. Who knew? We learned a lot of practical skills there. Did those make you nervous? Imagine the things I chose not to include!

A funny "only in Arkansas" experience happened on a trip to the city. Remember that city is still pretty small-town, so people are quite friendly. After shopping, when we were walking back to the truck in the parking lot, a car honked at Allen and Matt. So they went over to see what this older couple wanted. As I reached the truck, I heard the man say, "Hey, I have something to show you, but come around to this side." Because that didn't sound scary at all, Allen said, "Um, okay" and they did. The guy opened his door and said, "What do you think of that?!" Now I couldn't see from my vantage point, so I was dying of curiosity and just a little nervous. When Allen came back to the truck laughing, he filled me in. The man had pulled out his ... camouflage ... prosthetic leg. He'd said "I saw you two looking at the camo section back there and thought you'd get a kick out of this." (Props for that perfect pun!) Allen said, "Yep, it's awesome!" What else could he have said?

Once our chickens and ducks were doing well, we were ready to add some more animals to our unhomesteading life. And what are the cutest animals ever that everyone ought to have? Goats! With help from our tribe, we brought home Lucy, a three-day-old Alpine goat. We had to bottle-feed her and she was so adorable! That night, we realized she needed someone to sleep outside with her to keep her warm. Lizzy and Matt volunteered and spent the night in the goat pen with Lucy. It didn't go very well for Lizzy or Matt, but Lucy slept great.

According to our tribe, goats are very social and Lucy needed a playmate. So we brought home Annie, so named because it was our seventeenth wedding anniversary. This time it didn't go as smoothly. Annie was a few weeks old. She was a pretty Oberhasli who was tan with a black stripe. She had been with her mama and wasn't tame at all. Allen and the boys brought her home in a dog crate and put it in the goat pen. Once the goats got a little bigger, we planned to cover the windows in the pen, but thought we had a little time. Nope. Allen opened the crate and out came a scared but adorable little goat. Before he could move to block the window, Annie crashed right through it! She ran straight through the deer fence, into the garden, and back out, then off into the woods with Jack at her heels. It happened so fast we were all in shock! We chased her through the woods, but how do you catch a wild goat? I didn't even get a picture and Lizzy was inside, so she missed the whole ordeal.

There were coyotes, mountain lions, and bears on the mountain, so we didn't know how long she would make it. She wasn't even weaned yet, so we didn't know if she'd get enough food. Poor Annie. We were all so sad, and it happened on our anniversary too. It was just a hard day on the farm. And remember, we still had a little goat that needed company. Poor Lucy. But then our friend offered us another goat, until we figured out what to do. That cheered us all up a little. So Deuce joined the family. Deuce, because he was the second goat of the day! And he was adorable too.

Since it was the end of kidding season, we didn't think we'd be able to get another young goat. We wanted a young one, since the older goat didn't work out so well for us. And we really wanted another female for milk. So when our friend called and had a newborn, we were excited! We had covered the windows and fenced in the yard, so we were ready this time. So we met Lily, who had been born just a few hours earlier. She was part LaMancha, so she had the cute little ear nubs. We picked her up and she promptly fell asleep in Matt's arms. So now we had three goats on the farm.

In the first few days since Annie's escape, there were many sightings of "the elusive Lundy goat" whispered about on the mountain. We had awesome neighbors who spotted her and called to let us know. Some even attempted to catch her, but had no luck. Others had been on the lookout and prayed for her. We really appreciated our little mountain community! Allen and the boys went on goat hunts and we even used Deuce to try to call her in close to where she was last spotted, but nothing worked. After that first week, she hadn't been spotted much anymore. We were still hoping she was alive and would hear our goats or the neighbors' and eventually come in closer to eat. But since she was so young, it just wasn't possible. We knew, for quite some time, we would be the subject of conversations between the experienced homesteaders, as the newbies who lost the goat.

But twelve days later, in an amazing turn of events on the RVstead, the elusive goat was seen! Neighbors spotted her and let us know she was near an abandoned shack down the road. And it was raining, so we were hoping she would take shelter inside. Allen and the boys took ropes and went on another goat hunt. They sneaked stealthily up to the shack using hand signals, and they saw her! They surrounded the shack and blocked both entrances. Then they cornered her and tossed a rope around her neck! Annie put up a fight, but they got her and held on tight all the way home. When they pulled into the drive honking, I knew they had her! They wrestled her into the now reinforced pen, which was also now surrounded by a good fence! So after twelve days alone in the wild, our tough little Annie was home.

At first, Annie was very scared and wary of all of us, but she took to the other goats just fine. We took turns just sitting in the pen, hoping to get her used to people, but we knew it would take some time. She was eating well and appeared healthy, which was very impressive for a young goat that wasn't weaned yet or used to food or people! She didn't let us touch her for a few weeks, but soon enough she was as spoiled as the other three beggars who craved attention! So now we had four goats on the farm.

I still get the heebie jeebies thinking about what happened next. Just remember we're okay and it was a few years ago now. Allen wanted to show me the abandoned shack where they caught Annie, so I could see how it happened. We'd just hopped on the ATV and I was wearing flip flops, instead of my usual boots. Allen was walking through the dark room, recounting the events quite dramatically. He really likes to reenact events. So he was pointing out the exits they covered and where Annie was hiding, all the while weaving through the very narrow path through the room. He also picked up a cassette tape recorder, which showed the age of the shack. I was carefully stepping over decades of who knows what. Since it was dark, I had to lean over and look closely at each step too. Before one step, I leaned way down and noticed a coiled shape, with diamond markings and a triangle shaped head looking at me! It was about a foot from my face! I wish I could say I calmly jumped backwards, warned Allen of the snake, and left the shack. But I actually freaked out, tripped all over myself, squeaked out some high-pitched, indistinguishable noises, and ran out like I was on fire. While he didn't understand my noises, he knew from my reaction there must be a snake. So he quickly followed me out, coming back to step right over it! Again! Ugh. I honestly shudder still today when I think how close we both were. Even poor Annie could have run into it. Of course I wanted to leave immediately and of course Allen wanted to see the snake. While I stood on top of a box outside, dancing around and still trying to get higher, Allen went back inside. Then the rattling echoed through the little shack and it was so loud! Seriously, heebie jeebies. It did its job and warned us of the danger and then Allen did his job of convincing the snake to leave the mountain and never return. Allen can be very convincing. I got on the ATV and refused to stay any longer. We drove away and I never forgot to wear my boots again, ever.

Those near tragedies turned out well, but they didn't always. We lost a chicken occasionally to hawks or some other predator as they free ranged during the day. Once at night a raccoon reached into the coop and it wasn't pretty. And of course many of the animals went to freezer camp. Pause to think about that one if you need to. It's a nice way of saying they did their jobs as farm animals. But the kids learned this was part of farm life and adjusted very well. We were really sad one evening, though, because during the nightly chicken count, Jiffy Puff was missing. He was Matt's favorite chicken, who always wanted to be petted like a dog. Matt carried him everywhere around the farm. He was definitely more pet than working farm animal. We hoped he would turn up the next day like another chicken once had, but there was no Jiffy Puff. Poor Jiffy Puff. Poor Matt.

But two days later, Matt happened to open a toolbox and found him in there! And he was still alive! He was panting and quite filthy, though Josh's tools were even dirtier. It was really amazing because it was inside the barn and both days were over 100°F. There was no water, but there may have been a little cat food inside which held him over. We sometimes fed the cat in something up high so the chickens wouldn't steal her food. He must have hopped up there looking for food and it snapped shut on him. Jiffy Puff was stiff and slow for a little while, but after a long drink of water, he was just fine. We were so glad he was okay and Matt was especially happy!

Another happy occasion on the RVstead was when the Google Maps satellite finally flew over the mountain. There was an old image on there of vacant land and we hoped one day to see the barn and all the work we put into the land. Unfortunately, they didn't give us a warning or we would have picked up a little! On the image now, you can indeed see the barn, the RV, the fenced yard, and the mowed field. You can also see the truck out front with lumber in the back, as we were still working on the barn. And as usual, our laundry was hanging on the clothesline to dry. Do you understand the significance of this? It means you can see our underwear - from space!

One of the funniest events in Arkansas involved Matt, which isn't surprising. Allen and Matt went out squirrel hunting down the lake road and took the ATV. Allen dropped Matt off in one spot and went to another. He told Matt to be ready when he heard the ATV coming back. Since this was Lundy Mountain, they were obviously not going to run into anyone else. So Matt headed into the woods and pulled out his stool and his gun. He sat to watch and wait. After a while, he noticed a chigger on his arm, then another, then a few more. He looked down and realized his pants were covered! He pulled up his pants legs to find more. He lifted his shirt and they were all over him. Chiggers everywhere! Remember our chigger trauma? So he ran like crazy back to the road, shedding his clothes as he went. Fortunately, right then he heard the ATV, so he knew help was coming.

Imagine his surprise as he stood there, in only his underwear, holding a gun, waving as an older couple on ATVs drove by, laughing. Imagine their surprise, as they were driving down a road where they were obviously not going to run into anyone else, as they passed a cute, young, blond-haired boy, with a gun, waving politely at them, in only his underwear! They could have gone to the police station to file a report about a wild child who lives in the mountains alone, surviving on squirrels. But they probably went home assuming the best, telling a crazy tale of a half-naked boy in the woods!

After a long, fun season of unhomesteading, we decided to head back to Florida for the winter. We could have stayed in Arkansas. The RV was cozy warm, the pipes were heated, and the animals were comfy, but did we really want to? After a week of freezing temperatures and fun in the snow, we decided we definitely did not want to. Allen wanted to fish every day like the previous winter. We also really missed the grandparents, I had a retreat in Florida I couldn't miss, and well, it was too cold. We really prefer our winters to involve flip flops and sitting by the pool, while Allen's on the river catching dinner. Are we spoiled? Maybe. Are we lucky? No, we carefully planned our unhomesteading around our mobile life for just this reason.

So all of the farm animals either went to freezer camp or were swapped with neighbors for milk and eggs when we returned in the spring. It was a little hard to say goodbye to Jiffy Puff and another favorite, Chick Norris. They were pretty awesome, for chickens. But we knew they'd be with us, in our hearts and in our freezer.

We would certainly miss watching all the crazy animals, especially the goats. But since we traded them back to their original goat farm, we knew we'd get to visit them again, plus their future babies! That was a nice consolation. Those crazy goats are too easy to get attached to! So we planned to just have chickens and rabbits, when we returned in the spring.

We had a great winter in Florida, and as we emptied the freezer of meat, Allen filled it back up with fish. When we returned to Arkansas in the spring, our unhomesteading began again. We started with some new chicks and got our rabbits back from a neighbor. As we emptied the freezer of fish, we filled it back up with meat. The garden was also producing like crazy and we were eating a lot of it and canning the rest.

Things were going well, but the farm was just too quiet without the goats. So we borrowed Lucy and Lily back from their farm, just for the summer. Lucy was pregnant too, so we got to experience a goat birth. She was young and it wasn't an easy process, so it was a little scary. Lily kept nudging her head in comfort when she cried out. That was hard to hear, but she made it and had a cute little male we named Ace. Thanks to YouTube, Allen turned out to be a great goat midwife! He was a great help and mama and son were healthy and happy. Matt was unsure of the whole ordeal though, and wasn't very anxious to ever see that again.

You might be thinking you could never do that. Keep in mind, before that day, we had never done it either. We didn't even attend our own children's births, since they are all adopted! While we know the whole process of birth and new life is wonderful, we've just not been around it at all. So we had less experience than most, but we managed. We had the trailblazer tribe for advice and the internet for some graphic how-to videos. Hopefully you've seen our family doesn't have any extra luck or special talents. We're just willing to give things a try. If we can, truly anyone can! We knew nothing about unlocating, unschooling, undieting, or especially unhomesteading. We simply tried, learning as we went.

There's such freedom in just undoing what you think. We didn't think we could help a goat get through a tough birth, but that didn't matter. She needed us. We didn't think we could teach our kids at home, but that didn't matter. They needed us. You may not think you can do the thing you're thinking about right now, but that doesn't matter. Who needs you?

We had a lot of fun sharing our RVstead with some other families too. We'd put in an extra hook-up just for that purpose and it was quite entertaining to have neighbors experience our unhomesteading life in Arkansas. Just like our time parking on friends' farms, these RVing families had a great time letting their kids run free, enjoying the animals, and of course jumping on the trampoline. It was fun to share meals and conversations around the campfire again, which brought back the campground feeling we missed.

So the homestead was fun again, but also a lot of work again. As I mentioned, that second year of unhomesteading became really tiring. Instead of new and exciting, it just felt like unending chores. We were still learning and were definitely benefiting from the free meat and vegetables. But we decided we would rather travel again and let some other families enjoy the mountain. So we found renters who were ready for an adventure in Arkansas. As we explored the country, other RVing families got to experience unhomesteading. They all loved the area, learned a lot, and found that trailblazer tribe to help.

We made some mistakes on the RVstead, many in the garden. The first frost killed all of our dozens of tomato plants, because I wasn't prepared and started them too late. They were all still green, so I picked them and figured we'd learn if we liked fried green tomatoes or not. We ended up loving them! So I froze the rest for later and it wasn't much of a loss after all.

Another lesson you can learn from our mistakes is while deer netting is necessary around your garden, it will not stop chickens, cats, goats, or deer. Remember Annie? She ran straight through it. Use a stronger fence, reinforced with netting for the little critters, and move it far back from the garden. Our chickens loved our cucumbers. The goats ate half our green beans. The deer ate all of our corn. And the cat would just play with the tomatoes like little toys. Deer will also eat your fruit trees and expensive specialty hedges you order online, so protect those as well.

When gardening on a mountain, you will have rocks. Rocks weren't the mistake of course. Thinking we could get rid of them was. You can remove them, raise the beds, sift your dirt with screens, and use topsoil bought from a store, but it doesn't matter. Your husband will tell visitors "Rocks are our best crop." You'll laugh, but you will silently hate those rocks. Every time it rains, more rocks will come to the surface like magic. When you weed your garden, you will pull out more rocks than weeds. It's hard, but here is my advice based on experience. Don't throw the rocks out of anger. You will hit your chickens.

We didn't learn everything by mistake of course. And some things were really cool. For example, do you know how easy it is to make sour cream? You literally just take cream ... and let it sour. That blew my mind. We also learned to make yogurt, butter, whipped cream, and cheese. Those weren't as easy, but they were yummy.

We learned goats are always hungry. They are also always eating. They will actually "baa" with food in their mouths, choking on what they're eating, to let you know they need more. Goats are a lot like teenagers. Did you know in Japan, they spell the goat sound "meh" instead of "baa"? We think that's much closer, because ours definitely said "Maatt." Matt was the morning person to feed them and let them out. So every time they saw him, they would get excited and cry "Maatt" all day long.

Chickens taught us pecking order is a real thing, ruling the roost is a big deal, being cooped up is bad, having your eyes pecked out is really bad, and running around like a chicken with its head cut off is crazy. We learned so much from all the animals, projects, experiences, disasters, victories, and people during our unhomesteading adventures. I can't possibly share it all in this chapter. It would fill more than one book. I can't even share much advice, because homesteading really needs to be experienced personally.

I can encourage you, though, if you have any interest in homesteading, it doesn't have to be traditional. Just like home, work, or school, it doesn't have to be the way your neighbors expect. It doesn't have to be the way you expect. You can make it work for your family. You can just visit one, volunteer occasionally, or find regular work on a farm. Or you can find your mountain and try it out like we did. You can go all in and build your homestead. You can even design a fully self-sufficient earth ship from recycled material, with solar power, thermal heat, and a watering system for your garden from your shower. Just know you can do what you want, even if it looks more like unhomesteading than homesteading.

Keep in mind your homestead can be as calm, or as busy, as you'd like. If you're working on unscheduling, just be aware sometimes when people are offering you "help," they are actually offering you "busy." And if you're working on unschooling, you might notice sometimes people are promoting a class instead of an education. Usually the trailblazer tribe will help you with things you really need, like keeping your chickens alive, protecting your apple trees, or canning your blackberry jelly. Remember though, occasionally people won't be fulfilling your needs. They will be filling your calendar.

This same conversation has happened countless times over the years, and I've learned to just smile and nod.

Helper: "You homeschool? Well, there's this group and they meet on these dates and that activity and this event..."

Me: "Yes, but we like to keep it simple and enjoy life without being busy."

Helper: "But you have goats? They can show them at the fair and learn about their care and the breeds and they can get ribbons..."

Me: "Yes, but we like just having goats."

Busy people like to busy-up everyone else. And they are trying to be helpful. It's all they know. We just want to learn about goats (or anything else) simply because we need to know those things. We don't need to prove to anyone that we've learned properly. We don't need ribbons to show that we've done so. And we certainly don't want to complicate our lives with something we already do for fun!

Busyness does not mean fullness. Our life is very full, but very, very not busy. People frequently offer suggestions to help us stay busy. There are lots of good opportunities and they can be educational, beneficial, and fun, but are they really opportunities if they simply keep us busy? Not to us. We've chosen to keep our life full by not keeping it busy. Sometimes I start to wonder, maybe we should consider ... but then I look out the window and see a goat contentedly curled up in Matt's lap as they both watch deer grazing in the field. These are the moments I know we don't need 4-H, scouts, Homeschool Goat Care 101, or a curriculum ... sometimes we simply need a goat.

Margie Lundy

CHAPTER 11: UNLIMITING

You don't have to live in a house, go to school, work a traditional job, fill up your calendar, eat how you were raised to eat, only have friends in your local area, attend a local church, keep attached to the grid all the time, grow or hunt your own food the traditional way, or do anything the way your neighbor does it. Or how you were raised to do it. Or how your family expects you to do it. Or even how you think you should do it. You don't have to be limited. You can live the way you WANT to live. You can have that freedom.

I just read a comment yet again on an inspiring post. I see variations of it so often. It always says something like "Enjoy living your dream, because some of us can't." It always makes me so sad, because most of the time, they certainly can. They just don't know they can. I wish I could reach them all, shake them a little, and encourage them, "You can!"

If you dream of going to New Zealand, you can literally go buy a ticket and fly there. Yes, there are hurdles you'll have to jump. You'll have to save, plan, figure out if you should take the kids, ask off work or find a better job, find a dog sitter, rent your house or call in a favor, and a lot more. But it's not impossible. Allen and I flew to New Zealand for $800 each. How much did your couch cost? I'm not saying you have to go there, though it's gorgeous and we'd highly recommend it. I'm just saying you certainly can go there, if you want to make it happen. You might choose not to, for various reasons, but please don't think you can't.

I'm not going to tell you that you must believe in yourself, envision your perfect future, or clearly define your dream. Sometimes you just need to buy a ticket. It certainly can be valuable to believe, envision, and dream and we do that often. But sometimes people use that as an excuse. It can be overwhelming and abstract. Sometimes you just need to take that step into the un-known. The help will come.

If you want a new job, it's not your lack of belief stopping you. It's probably that you haven't applied for one. If you want to take a vacation, you don't need to wait on your perfect future where you have more time and money. You just need to stop spending money so you can save enough for a vacation. If you want to do something special with your family, you don't need to wait until you have your life goals laminated to see what activities would resonate with them. You just need to pick something and do it.

Life really can be simple and there's great freedom in that. You are not limited to what you have or think you can have. If you don't have something you want, make a plan to get it. If there's something you want to change, make a plan to change it. You may need to undo everything you think, but that will bring you the freedom you desire. And that freedom is not one day having more money, time, health, travel, fulfillment, adventure, family, influ-ence, education, or faith. True freedom is realizing you can have all of those right now, if you just rethink everything.

ACKNOWLEDGEMENTS

This book wouldn't be possible without my family or my tribes – literally, it's about them. :)

Allen, my husband, partner, best friend, and adventure guide, thank you for loving me, putting up with me, entertaining me, and pushing me way past my comfort zone. Josh, you bring unrivaled enthusiasm to any endeavor. Matt, your humor makes me laugh, but also makes me crazy. You boys are always up for any adventure and you make things fun, if a little scary. Lizzy, you are rarely up for an adventure, but always say yes anyway. And you still kick butt and make us proud. I couldn't choose a better family to continually risk my life with. Thank you. ♥

To my tribes, from the chapters in this book and ones that may never be written, thank you for your love and for always gathering in support. You make the hard things bearable and the easy things fun.

From my nomadic, adoption, and health tribes, thanks so much to Tiana Johnson, Jennie Ennis-Mason, and Julie L. Szymankowski for your valuable input and help with this book.

To the trailblazers, thank you for unthinking everything.

ABOUT THE AUTHOR

Margie Lundy is a nomadic explorer, wife, mom, author, unschooler, photographer (not a good one), coach, and finder of anything. She loves God, family, and adventure, in that order. Margie doesn't use her physics degree, studies the effects of trauma on brain development in her spare time, and lives and teaches healthy nutrition, while acknowledging that chocolate is imperative to happiness.

She is currently on the road somewhere with her family. Follow their adventures and download a free guide, "Where to Start on the Road to Freedom", at www.unlocating.com.
If you'd like to chat, give feedback, or ask questions, email Margie at author@unlocating.com.

RESOURCES

Here are some great websites to learn about life on the road. If you're interested in unlocating, unworking, unschooling, unscheduling, unfriending, or unplugging, check them out!

Fulltime Families has many resources, videos, and stories for RVing families.
www.fulltimefamilies.com

The Fulltime Families Facebook group is where over 30,000 people connect and share.
www.facebook.com/groups/FulltimeFamilies

Technomadia provides helpful resources that include jobs, community, mail, healthcare, WiFi, and more.
www.technomadia.com/excuses

Xscapers is a working-age community with passion for an active and free-spirited life of travel and adventure.
www.xscapers.com

And of course you'll find valuable resources on our website, including a **free** guide, "Where to Start on the Road to Freedom."
www.unlocating.com

NOTE FROM THE AUTHOR

Thanks for coming along on this Unlocating journey with me. I truly hope you enjoyed it!

Will you consider leaving a short review on Amazon? Even just a few words would help others decide if this book is right for them. Your help is greatly appreciated.

You may also share on Good Reads, Facebook, Twitter, Instagram, or Pinterest.

Thank you! ♥

Margie Lundy
www.unlocating.com
www.facebook.com/unlocating

END NOTES

[1] Merriam-Webster. "Tribe." 2019, www.merriam-webster.com/dictionary/tribe.

[2] Proctor, Bob. "Law of Vibration." *Proctor Gallagher Institute*, 2015, www.proctorgallagherinstitute.com/6956/the-law-of-vibration.

[3] *Band of Brothers*. Directed by Phil Alden Robinson, et al. DreamWorks, HBO Films, 2001.

[4] Lundy, Josh. "The army is so panfull." Miami East Kindergarten, Ohio, 2006.

[5] Fetteroll, Joyce. "Definition of Unschooling." Facebook, 2018, www.facebook.com/groups/unschoolquotearama.

[6] National Park Service. Junior Ranger Program. www.nps.gov/kids/jrrangers.cfm.

[7] Dodd, Sandra. "Can it Work in the Real World?" (n.d.), www.sandradodd.com/unschooling.

[8] Learn Liberty. "On Tyrants & Tributes- Real World Lessons From The Hunger Games." 2014, www.learnliberty.org.

[9] Merriam-Webster. "Socialization." 2019, www.merriam-webster.com/dictionary/socialization.

[10] Dictionary.com. "Socialized." 2019, www.dictionary.com/browse/socialized.

[11] Godin, Seth. *Linchpin: Are You Indispensable?* First Edition, Portfolio, 2010.

[12] Dodd, Sandra. "Quotes for Unschoolers." (n.d.), www.sandradodd.com/quotes.

[13] Fetteroll, Joyce. "Quotes for Unschoolers." (n.d.), www.sandradodd.com/quotes.

[14] Dingmann, Amy. "Dear Homeschoolers, Please Stop. Part 2." (n.d.), www.thehmmmschoolingmom.com/homeschoolers-please-stop-part-two.

[15] Gatto, John Taylor. Twitter, 2017, www.twitter.com/realjohngatto/status/942959952619900928.

[16] Hardy, Darren. "Darren Daily." 2019, www.darrendaily.com.

[17] Jacks, L.P. *Education Through Recreation*. First Edition, Harper & Brothers, 1932.

[18] Disputed quote. Rogers, Kenny (attributed 1990) or Rockefeller, John D (attributed 2006). en.wikiquote.org/wiki/John_D._Rockefeller.

[19] Ramsey, Dave. "Dave Ramsey's 7 Baby Steps." (n.d.), www.daveramsey.com/dave-ramsey-7-baby-steps.

[20] Paine, Crystal. "Money Saving Mom." 2019, www.moneysavingmom.com.

[21] Hohlbaum, Christine Louise. *The Power of Slow: 101 Ways to Save Time in Our 24/7 World.* First edition, St. Martin's Griffin, 2009.

[22] Covey, Stephen. *The 7 Habits of Highly Effective People.* First edition, Simon & Schuster, 1989.

[23] Google Dictionary. "Nomad." 2019, www.google.com/search?q=define+nomad.

[24] Google Dictionary. "Community." 2019. www.google.com/search?q=define+community.

[25] *National Lampoon's Christmas Vacation.* Directed by Jeremiah Chechik. Performance by Chevy Chase. Warner Bros., Hughes Entertainment, 1989.

[26] Lemaster, Deny. Facebook. 2019, www.facebook.com/deny.lemaster.

[27] Jacobsen, Wayne. *Finding Church: What If There Really Is Something More?* First edition, TrailView Media, 2014.

[28] Wikipedia. "Homesteading." 2019, en.wikipedia.org/wiki/Homesteading.

Made in the USA
Las Vegas, NV
19 December 2021

38709701R00080